Putting Analysis into Assessment

Undertaking assessments of need – a toolkit for practitioners

Ruth Dalzell and Emma Sawyer

NCB's vision is a society in which all children and young people are valued and their rights are respected. By advancing the well-being of all children and young people across every aspect of their lives, NCB aims to:

- reduce inequalities in childhood
- ensure children and young people have a strong voice in all matters that affect their lives
- promote positive images of children and young people
- enhance the health and well-being of all children and young people
- encourage positive and supportive family, and other environments.

NCB has adopted and works within the UN Convention on the Rights of the Child.

Published by the National Children's Bureau

National Children's Bureau, 8 Wakley Street, London EC1V 7QE
Tel: 020 7843 6000
Website: www.ncb.org.uk
Registered charity number: 258825

NCB works in partnership with Children in Scotland (www.childreninscotland.org.uk) and Children in Wales (www.childreninwales.org.uk).

© National Children's Bureau 2011

ISBN: 978 1 907969 29 4

Second edition published 2011
First edition published 2007

British Library Cataloguing in Publication Data
A catalogue record for this book is available from the British Library

Typeset by Saxon Graphics Ltd, Derby
Printed in UK by Hobbs the Printers Ltd, Totton, Hampshire SO40 3WX

Contents

Foreword

The uncertainties, demands and complexities that attend child safeguarding practice are as pronounced now as they ever have been. Practice is inherently charged with high risk, tension and emotion and involves professionals making finely balanced judgements about children in very difficult circumstances. To make thorough, well-founded, good quality assessments requires practitioners to be adept at gathering, synthesising and analysing large quantities of information from a range of sources, making sense of it and reaching conclusions to inform decisions with potentially far-reaching consequences. Professionals need formal knowledge and high level skills and expertise in practice.

The original project 'Putting Analysis into Assessment' and the publication of the same name sought to find ways to support social workers and their managers to continuously develop and hone their skills and confidence through providing them with information, tools and resources and inviting them to create the opportunities in their practice and organisation for learning and reflection.

Professor Eileen Munro's most welcome and thorough analytical review of Child Protection has once again highlighted the complexities of child protection and of the importance of continuous development of expertise. This toolkit is a significant aid to this.

The continuing popularity of the first edition of the toolkit and the evident thirst for opportunities to acquire knowledge and expertise tells us that this resource is of enduring value. It has been updated to reflect changes in policy and some new developments in research and practice but the core messages remain the same. I hope that the new edition will help to contribute to the development of even greater professional expertise in assessment and analysis and most importantly to improved outcomes for children and young people.

Sheryl Burton
Programme Director, Vulnerable Children
National Children's Bureau

Acknowledgements

The Putting analysis into assessment project was funded by Department for Education.

We would like to thank the managers and practitioners from the teams in Wandsworth and Leicestershire Children's Services departments for their participation in the project, and for sharing their ideas and experiences. Their feedback has informed the development of this toolkit.

Thanks also to Advisory Group members who gave generously of their time and expertise in the planning, development and undertaking of the project:

Julie Barnes, Independent Consultant
Jenny Gray, Professional Advisor, Children's Safeguards Policy Unit, DfES
Val Rogers, Sector Manager, Safeguarding and Commissioning, Wandsworth Social Services
Wendy Rose (Chair), Senior Research Fellow, The Open University
Jane Scannell, Service Manager, Children and Young People's Service, Leicestershire County Council
Dr Janet Seden, Senior lecturer, Faculty of Health and Social Care, The Open University
Jane Wiffin, Freelance Trainer and Senior Lecturer, PQCCA University of Bedfordshire
Laura Williams, Social Work Manager, Wandsworth Social Services (Children and Families Division).

We would also like to thank the following speakers at regional events and seminars relating to the project: Eileen Munro (London School of Economics), Jan Horwath (University of Leicester), Diana Bourn (University of Leicester), Steve Walker (Royal Holloway, University of London), Moraene Roberts (ATD Fourth World) and Danielle Turney (Open University).

And thanks also to the practitioners and managers who attended the training courses that were developed following the project, and gave us feedback relating to the tools in this toolkit.

Finally, we would like to thank colleagues at NCB who provided input, ideas and support with the project and with this publication: Diane Hart, Joanna McCann, Alison Williams, Jane Powell, Sheryl Burton, Kate Thomas and Stephen Howell.

Dedication

The National Children's Bureau and Leicestershire County Council would like to acknowledge the contribution of Anne Brown, Children's Planning Officer, Leicestershire Social Services, whose enthusiasm and vision for this project was instrumental in its success. This publication is dedicated to her memory.

Introduction

Who is the toolkit for?

This toolkit has been written with the needs of social work practitioners and managers in mind, but it will also be useful to other professionals who are involved in assessing the needs of children and families. It is a practical resource, intended to provide tools and ideas to enhance analytical thinking by those undertaking assessments.

How can it be used?

A range of materials are provided within the book that are designed to: aid practitioners in their thinking before, during and at the conclusion of their work with children and families; provide managers with materials that can be used in supervision and practice development activities within the team; and provide trainers with suggested material and programmes for delivering training to those involved in social work and inter-agency assessments.

The book can be read from cover to cover or readers can go straight to sections and tools that are of interest or practical use in supporting their needs. Within each of the sections that contain resources and tools, there is a discussion about the tool's purpose, its relevance and possible uses, along with a case study and practice development session to demonstrate its use in practice.

The PowerPoint presentations accompanying this publication can be downloaded from www.ncb.org.uk/resources/support. The presentations can be used in team-development or training courses. Suggested programmes for one and two-day training courses can also be downloaded. These programmes have all been tested in practice and have received positive feedback.

What is in the toolkit?

The pack is divided into three main areas, the assessment in context, practical resources and moving forward.

Chapter 1 offers an introductory discussion about the importance of analysis within the social work task; the need to raise standards in this area; the relevant wider context in which social workers are operating; and describes the Putting analysis into assessment project, from which this toolkit has emerged.

Chapters 2, 3 and 4 outline resources and tools to help practitioners preparing for assessment, planning and conducting the assessment, making decisions and drawing conclusions, and reporting findings. Chapter 5 offers activities to assist with considering the culture of analysis within a team or agency.

Chapter 6 considers the importance of team and agency culture further, discussing inter-agency issues and the opportunities and challenges there are for developing a more evidence-based and analytical approach within the social work task. It includes discussion on related issues such as what aids and hinders practitioners in being analytical; and what teams and agencies can do to support analytical practice. It also covers some discussion of wider issues, such as the interaction between social services and the court system; the impact of societal expectations on social workers; and the realities of trying to undertake complex, reflective work in the context of time and resource pressures.

Training course materials, such as presentations, and suggested training programmes can be downloaded from www.ncb.org.uk/resources/support.

Since the publication of the 1st edition of the toolkit in 2007, both authors have delivered training to a multitude of practitioners from social work and across the wider children's services. The consistently well-received materials from the 1st edition of the toolkit, sometimes with small adjustments, have remained in this 2nd edition, new materials have been produced to reflect the developing evidence base for current practice themes and to take into account messages for practice from *The Munro Review of Child Protection* (Munro 2011).

1. The assessment process in context

Background

The Framework for the Assessment of Children in Need and their Families (Department of Health and others 2000) otherwise known as The Assessment Framework was developed to assess the needs of children under the Children Act 1989. It provides a systematic way of analysing, understanding and recording what is happening to children and young people, both within their families and in the wider context of the community in which they live, in order to be able to make professional judgements. These judgements include: whether the child is in need, or is suffering significant harm; what actions should be taken; and what services would best meet the needs of the particular child and family.

The Assessment Framework was intended to ensure that referral and assessment processes discriminate effectively between different types and levels of need; there is a timely service response to identified needs; and, in turn, better outcomes for children.

Although the intentions of the Children Act 1989 were to identify children in need and provide services to meet their needs, research studies – commissioned by the Department of Health (DH) and summarised in *Child Protection: Messages from research* (1995) – showed that child protection concerns continued to be the main trigger by which families gained access to services. In many authorities, it was only when there was evidence of potential significant harm to a child that access to family support services could be gained. This was the direct opposite of the intentions of Part 3 of the Act. The absence of a consistent approach nationally to the assessment of children in need meant that similar children were being treated very differently in different authorities.

The Assessment Framework takes the broad approach to identifying children in need, as intended by the Children Act 1989 and is designed to be used as a working tool for social workers and others involved in inter-agency assessments. The triangle of the assessment framework with its three domains: the child's developmental needs; the capacity of parents to meet those needs; and the impact of family, community and environmental factors, is now widely accepted across the range of agencies. There is no doubt that The Assessment Framework has improved and standardised practice across England. However, messages from inspections and research have regularly identified that analysis continues to be a major area of concern for practice.

The report '*Learning Lessons, Taking Action: Ofsted's evaluations of serious case reviews 1*' (Dec. 2008), highlighted failings in practice, indicative of poor analysis including a failure to consider the impact of parental issues on children, responding reactively to information rather than taking a long-term view and taking what parents said at face value rather than speaking directly to children.

Similarly, Turney and others' review for DFE *Social Work Assessment of Children in Need. What do we know – Messages from research* (2011) states:

> It is clear from the studies we reviewed that the analysis of information has continued to be problematic in practice so attention needs to be focused on strengthening this crucial aspect of the assessment process.

Amongst a number of commonly identified barriers to good analytical assessment practice, one in particular has been at the heart of recent debate. The Integrated Children's System (ICS) introduced by the government in 2004 was intended to create an electronic case management system that provided a common conceptual and recording framework from the point of early concerns through referral, assessment, planning for children in need and in protection, in care, and moving into independence.

Whilst originally welcomed in principle by most as an opportunity to modernise and unify previously disjointed processes and create a common language throughout the system, it has proved to be overambitious, complex, unwieldy and difficult to implement. Bell, Shaw and Sinclair (2007) commented that the more ambitious a programme the greater the problems associated with its implementation; and the stories of problems with ICS implementation certainly support this view.

Practitioners in Bell, Shaw and Sinclair's study reported finding the system too prescriptive with the potential for duplication of information and too many tick boxes. Practitioners on training sessions run by the authors of this book frequently bemoan the gap between the practice they aspire to and the reality of a system that allows miniscule amounts of time to engage with children, which requests information under tightly prescribed headings and which often produces long disjointed reports that make little sense to families.

Numerous observers have also scrutinised the impact of prescribed timescales for assessments within ICS. Widely shared concerns are neatly summed up by Helm (2010).

> *The creation of such timescales, while beneficial in terms of accountability and avoidance of 'drift', can also create difficulties when the goal for practitioners and organizations becomes the meeting of timescales, and this has a higher priority than the submission of an assessment that provides appropriate levels of analysis built upon a meaningful dialogue with children and their families.*

The difficulties with ICS have been put down variously to lack of capacity in the IT marketplace, a failure to grasp the best of new technology, lack of investment in training and support and human failings such as lack of skills in operating computerised systems. Perhaps by trying too hard to capture everything, ICS has unintentionally hindered rather than encouraged the development of creative, confident and competent practice.

However, the chorus of dissatisfaction with ICS should not obscure the potential benefits of having a coherent and unified recording system.

In 2010 the government commissioned Professor Eileen Munro to undertake a review of Child Protection in England. In the 2011 final report of the review Professor Munro described the current child protection system as over-bereaucratised and focused on compliance, and as a defensive system that emphasises procedures over the development of expertise. Munro calls for the development of a system that prioritises 'doing the right thing' (checking whether children are being helped) over 'doing things right' (following procedures).

Munro recommends amongst other things a reduction in the amount of central prescription, including the removal of timescales for assessment, revision of statutory guidance and greater investment in the development of professional expertise.

Despite the contribution that ICS may or may not have made to the erosion of social work expertise we would probably easily agree with the essential skills of social work described succinctly in The 12th Annual report of the Chief Inspector of Social Services (Department of Health 2003).

> *Time and again the role of skilled social worker, in supporting, befriending and analysing the family has been found to be critical to the outcome for the child.*

Analysing information in a way that makes the process transparent and able to be explained to a broad audience is no easy task and is challenging for a range of professionals, not just social workers. This book focuses on analysis because it is such an essential and integral part of the social work task and is the process upon which decisions about children's welfare, within and after assessments, hinge. Before considering some of the specific challenges of social work analysis, it is important to define what is meant by 'analysis' in this context. A definition is important because when a practitioner is gathering information, reviewing what they know and making a decision, it is difficult for them to identify what part of the process constitutes 'analysis'. It is hardly surprising then, that social work decisions often take some explaining and justifying to service users, other professionals and in courts. In truth, analysis occurs throughout the whole assessment process – it influences whether assessments are carried out in the first place; and the decisions, however small, about how to go about them, who to involve and what information to gather.

Dictionary definitions of the words assessment and analysis suggest that they should in theory be comfortable bedfellows. Assessment means to appraise, measure, estimate or give consideration to a situation, whilst analysis means to examine, study, and break down into simpler elements.

It should therefore follow that in order to carry out a proper assessment of any situation, a certain amount of analysis needs to be undertaken. When faced with a complex situation one usually gathers all the facts and gives them consideration, separately and in relation to one another. This might be done by breaking down the information into simpler elements or manageable chunks under headings, then weighing up the options. For example, a parent choosing a school for their child might gather information about which schools are available within travelling distance of where they live. They would then find out what they could about each school, asking certain questions determined by their individual priorities: Is the school more geared towards the arts, sciences or sports? How does this match with their child's needs or indeed their aspirations for him or her? What is the academic record of the school and what are its policies and record on pastoral care, bullying and discrimination? Is it convenient for local bus routes or walking to school and what is their child's preference? Would their child be able to transfer with existing friends or make friends they could socialise with outside of school?

The parent would then analyse the information gathered, which would require a certain amount of weighting of the different options. Is an easy journey to school more important than the school record in sports for example? This would lead ultimately to the decision that, hopefully, was right for their child and for them. As any parent who has been through this process knows, this is not a pain-free activity and it is hard. There are some gains and losses and some likely compromise in any decision that is made. In many human situations there are also too many variables to ever be certain that the decision made is the 'right' one. Many of the factors that will contribute to the experience that the child has at school will be outside the parent's control, so the parent can only ever hope to make the best choice out of a range of available options at that given time. Important as the decision in the above example undoubtedly is, it may seem rather straightforward when compared with some of the practice judgements and decisions required by social workers trying to support children and families living in the most challenging circumstances. Deciding how to protect and promote good outcomes for children – when they are living, for example, with parents with mental health or substance misuse problems, helping parents with learning disabilities to understand the needs of their children or trying to assess the likelihood of significant harm occurring to a child living in poverty or in the context of chronic neglect – throw up huge challenges for workers trying to reach a balanced view in the knowledge that decisions that they make could have a massive and enduring impact on a child's future health, well-being and family relationships.

In much the same way that the parent choosing a school for their child may have to settle for a decision that seems the 'best option' given all that they know; social workers, when dealing with such complex and unpredictable variables, can only hope to draw conclusions that are the 'least likely to be wrong' (Holland 2004). They must strive to do all they can to ensure that decisions and recommendations are made with rigorous checks and balances to counteract their human tendencies (to be influenced by time pressures, anxiety, false optimism or negative judgements).

So what makes the desired standard of analytical practice so elusive and difficult to achieve? Well, as discussed earlier, the decisions to be made are by no means easy. The use of evidence from research and theoretical approaches can support the task, but how far can these be generalised to individual situations and how confident can busy practitioners be in their acquisition and application of knowledge from such sources?

How much time is there to be reflective? As one social worker in the Putting analysis into assessment project commented:

> You don't tend to have a pen and paper to hand when you reflect, as it is more likely to occur when you are doing something else, such as driving or washing up!

In fact, can a form – even guidelines, checklists or complex equations – show us how to be analytical? To what extent is analysis an intuitive creative skill that you've either got or you haven't? Theories about human decision-making abound; and some of these have been explored in the context of social work decision-making specifically by, for example, Eileen Munro (2008), Sally Holland (2004), and Ann Hollows (2003). These complex arguments are not explored in great depth in this toolkit, but they have been drawn upon to identify practical approaches for helping social workers to make judgements. These approaches were tested, with social workers, as part of the Putting analysis into assessment project (described on page 7); and their experiences are shared in Chapters 2 and 3. Also covered are some of the factors identified by practitioners as having a bearing on the nature and quality of analysis in their assessments. First, however, it is important to consider the context within which social workers are operating, so as to take it into account when examining the many influences on their thinking, decision-making and capacity to be analytical.

Wider context

Social work with children and families does not operate in a vacuum. Practice is influenced by a whole range of a social and cultural norms and traditions. Definitions of childhood and child abuse are socially constructed, varying over time, and approaches to social work practice have been subject to rather more influence from fashion than perhaps some other professions.

> Practitioners ... are working within a field of evolving knowledge and changing public attitudes and expectations. Often they can find themselves at the forefront of discovery without the support of established knowledge.
>
> (Butler and Williamson 1994 p.10)

The unprecedented attention given to improving public services by the last government has impacted perhaps more on services for children than in any other area. The Every Child Matters Programme (2004) led to wholesale changes in the organisation, delivery and inspection of children's services. At the heart of these changes was an expressed wish to increase the focus on the child and ensure that their voice was clearly heard in decisions made for and about them. The Every Child Matters Programme was informed by messages from research relating to outcomes for children plus a national consultation process with young people but it is also important to remember that this took place in the context of developments in wider society. Recent years have seen changes in the concept and means of exercising customer power and influence and customer consultation and feedback are now regarded as a core activity for assuring a quality service. From motor vehicle repairs to evening classes it sometimes feels as though the feedback form has developed a life of its own. All this frenetic activity is aimed at improving the service being offered. Cynics may say that these systems have more to do with being able to tick boxes to achieve a level of self-satisfaction than improving the service offered but it is fair to say that this culture is accompanied by a desire to put those at the receiving end of services in a more central position. Moreover, it has led to greater transparency of decision-making and a need for processes to be more open to scrutiny and examination.

Most would agree, that The Assessment Framework, The Common Assessment Framework, The Integrated Children's System and other recent developments in policy and legislation have come out of genuine attempts to improve practice and outcomes for children. It could be argued, however, that these ideas are not so much new as a reconfiguration of existing ideas, reflecting the holistic, preventive practice that social workers, in coordination with other agencies, have striven to achieve for many years. However one sees it, there is no doubt that whilst the rhetoric, expectations and potential models that surround the social work task remain the focus of constant debate, this, along with the fear and pressure generated by tragedies and public responses to them (which invariably spur such debates), can be seen as potentially undermining practitioners' confidence and their ability to focus on the task in hand.

It is of course not the intention of such initiatives to undermine practice; instead they are moves towards improved practice, which are largely positive and create important opportunities. If social workers and others who share responsibility for assessing and responding to the needs of vulnerable children and families are to be supported in doing so effectively, they need the systems within which they operate to enable this, which is the aim of these initiatives. However, the simple but very real difficulties practitioners face in finding the time, space and resources to enable them to reflect on their work also have to be addressed – in ways that policy and initiatives are unlikely to achieve alone. The culture of the team or agency that practitioners work within, the expectations they have of each other and that their managers have of them, all need to allow priority to be given to practitioners taking time to think carefully and to record this thinking usefully.

Putting analysis into assessment project

In response to the identified need for improvement in analysis within social work assessments, the National Children's Bureau undertook a project funded by the Department for Education and Skills (DfES) called Putting analysis into assessment, which ran from 2003 to 2005. The tools and approaches outlined in this pack were tested within the course of the project.

The project aimed to improve the assessment of children and families by working directly with social work practitioners and managers to enhance their skills in analysis and to help them understand the basis for their judgements, to encourage a focus on outcomes for children and to explore how professional confidence and knowledge might be improved.

The project worked in depth with two local authorities, in their children and families teams, and involved practitioners and managers in other areas through seminars and workshops at a regional and national level. For the four social work teams directly involved in the project, participation entailed a combination of engaging in and receiving feedback on case audits, practitioner interviews and questionnaires plus engagement in monthly practice development sessions over a nine month period and opportunities to attend seminars with expert speakers such as Professor Eileen Munro from London School of Economics, Jan Horwath from the University of Sheffield and Steve Walker from Royal Holloway, University of London.

Both the participating local authorities had recent three star ratings and the teams were front-line teams engaged in initial or core assessments or both. One of the authorities was a highly urban London borough with a high staff turnover whereas the other was a county council with a stable workforce in the Midlands.

Early discussions with team managers revealed some common themes across the teams, such as:

- varying levels of confidence in completing core assessments
- an awareness of, and desire, to implement the practice recommendations from the Laming Inquiry into the death of Victoria Climbie
- a lack of reference to research and the wider evidence base in assessment reports
- a view of the assessment, by some, as simply a route to accessing resources, or as a requirement for a child protection case conference.

An in-depth analysis, which was also evident in the reports, revealed a number of key issues concerning practitioners.

- There was some lack of confidence in responding to specific issues.
- It was felt that there were few opportunities for teams to reflect together on practice issues and challenges.
- There was concern over level of involvement of other professionals in the assessment process.
- Although supervision took place and was generally supportive, it could be rather functional.
- Some practitioners were confident in drawing on some theories, namely child development and attachment, but were less confident about directly referring to theory or research in assessment reports.
- There were numerous challenges in maintaining a focus on needs and outcomes, including difficulties in engaging parents and other practitioners, lack of time and the dangers of resource led recommendations.
- Children were often presented in a two dimensional way – their authentic voices were rarely used and the methods of ascertaining their wishes and feelings not reported.
- An analysis of culture and identity issues were often absent from many reports.
- There was a desire for more in-depth training and development activities that went beyond the basic one or two day course.

All participants felt there was room for increasing their knowledge and confidence in order to improve their analytical skills, but that lack of time, volume of work and the challenging nature of the work make it difficult to be analytical and reflective – both of which are essential to good decision-making.

By the end of the project, through being introduced to tools and ideas to assist them in thinking about cases, decisions and their ability to analyse, participants in the main felt they had benefited in terms of their confidence and capacity to be analytical. The reflection required and discussion time allowed during the project was itself a key factor in this.

2. Preparing for and planning assessments

The activities in this chapter are to assist practitioners in becoming more analytical before and during the planning and preparation stages of assessments, although the materials themselves could be used at any stage in the assessment process.

Preparing oneself: The reflective mindset

This section looks at the importance of developing a critical and reflective mindset and examines some of the arguments about how people think and make decisions. It looks at the importance of emotion in decision-making; and introduces a practice tool designed to help practitioners understand the influences on their own decision-making and the nature of expertise.

Reflective mindset

Analysis not only happens at the end of the assessment. It could be argued that, in addition to happening throughout the assessment process, it needs to start before the case is even referred. Applying a more analytical approach to assessment requires the practitioner to have already begun developing a critical and reflective mindset; and so be ready to approach the task in an attentive manner.

Reder and Duncan (1999) refer to this as the development of a *dialectic* mindset. This concept has been around since the teachings of Socrates and follows the principles of promoting 'the acquisition of knowledge through dialogue and argument'. This idea has much in common with the concept of reflective practice. Moon (1999) describes reflective practice as follows.

> *A set of abilities and skills to indicate the taking of a critical stance, an orientation to problem solving or state of mind.*

Schön contributed significantly to the notion of *reflecting on experience* to improve action in professional practice; firstly, through work on learning organisations and latterly, through his work on the reflective practitioner (Schön 1983) and the notion of reflection-in-action or, put more simply, 'thinking on our feet'. This involves looking to our experiences, connecting with our feelings and attending to the theories in use. It entails building new understandings to inform our actions in the situation that is unfolding.

Holland (2004) refers to reflection, which she describes as 'critical thoughtfulness' about practice experience before, during and after practice events. She also introduces the more complex notion of *reflexivity*, which she describes as a 'fundamental examination of the discourses and knowledge systems that underpin interactions in social, care'. Reflective or even reflexive practice is an aspiration for most social workers but may seem a somewhat esoteric goal in the cut and thrust of team life. In reality, it is something that needs to be supported on a variety of different levels; individual, team and agency, and which requires careful nurturing and the time and space to thrive.

Practitioners and team managers gave feedback, during the Putting analysis into assessment project, that the impact upon people's ability to be more thoughtful and reflective was one of the most significant benefits of the practice development work in teams. It seems to have been the introduction of the notion of thinking more critically or thinking about how we think, combined with the space created for the team to reflect together at the same time that brought about this change. The following comments, made by practitioners during the project evaluation, support this.

> *The project has affected assessments, evaluations and reasons for decisions are more confident/thought through.*

> *As a team we discuss more cases/practice share ideas, examine existing assessments more thoroughly, the team has benefited from spending project sessions together.*

> *We appreciated time away from casework responsibilities for personal development to benefit case work.*

The project created an opportunity for individual practitioners to reflect on the influences on their own practice and on decisions that had been made, in a safe and supportive way within the team. Being able to do this, over a period of time with an external facilitator, contributed to the development of a habit of doing this within supervision and peer discussion – a habit that was still apparent several months after the fieldwork had been completed. This could be described as a kind of 'priming', which is akin to 'learning to learn' as described by Caxton (1999).

Intuition and analysis

One of the areas that the Putting analysis into assessment project concentrated on was increasing understanding of the role, place and strengths and weaknesses of both analysis and intuition in social work decision-making. These can often be the subject of polarised, somewhat sterile debates so the project sought to promote a more balanced, integrated approach with both intuitive and analytical skills being seen as essential and interdependent in practice.

Intuitive thinking tends to be the way in which most people operate innately. O'Sullivan (1999) suggests that although intuition is often seen as an important aspect of professional decision-making, its definition and nature are problematic. O'Sullivan points out that the absence of deliberation in intuitive decision-making means that it is a relatively quick way of making use of limited information by sensing patterns and filling in gaps. He suggests that professional intuition is something that develops through experience and cannot be formally taught. As Munro points out however, 'experience on its own is not enough. It needs to be allied to reflection' Munro (2011).

Munro (2002) discusses the analytical–intuitive divide in social work and relates this to the broader debates contained in theories of decision-making over the centuries. She explores the strengths and weaknesses of both approaches: highlighting the fact that intuitive thinking is a largely unconscious process which is key to the way people make sense of the world; being swift, simple and drawing on imagination, empathy, gut feelings and past experience. She also makes the point that it is often an unreliable approach, which is flawed as a source of public knowledge as it is difficult to articulate, prone to bias, relies on narrow samples and is limited by personal experience.

In contrast to this, analytical thinking is a 'step by step, conscious, logically defensible process' (Hammond 1996), which is focused on breaking decisions down into elements, which are then carefully considered in relation to each other.

Analysis, according to Munro (2002), is based on empirical research and a much wider knowledge base that has been tested and is open to public scrutiny. Many aspects of a subject have been studied and, due to the wide availability of research databases nowadays, comprehensive overviews of research studies are available. Munro sounds a note of caution with regard to analytical and actuarial[1] approaches and states that, in some areas, there is still a limited knowledge base; that findings are often only tentative at best; and that trying to apply research findings across populations can be dangerous. Findings cannot be viewed uncritically – human judgement is still a critically important element.

Research by Dreyfus and Dreyfus (1986, referred to in Munro 2002 p.26) found that, in practice, clinicians begin by relying heavily on the analytical actuarial tools and then, over time, gradually integrate these into their thinking so that they are eventually drawing on them unconsciously. She points out that this is somewhat different in the case of social work, as social workers often start out by drawing on a lot of folk psychology. She makes the following point.

> Child protection workers need to become more analytical and critical to improve accuracy – make reasoning more open and accountable. The centrality of empathy and intuition needs to be acknowledged but practice can be improved by developing professionals' analytical skills.

O'Sullivan (1999) likewise suggests that social workers need to know how to go about analysis whilst at the same time developing their intuitive expertise, as both intuition and analysis have an important role in social work.

Jones and others (2006) discuss the importance of applying an evidence base thoughtfully and critically; and the limitations of trying to apply it in a precise or numerical way due to the complexity of the interaction of factors in human situations . The evidence base in question is one comprising factors associated with future harm in situations where a child has previously suffered harm. They stress that the process of decision-making needs to be as open as possible from an ethical as well as a practical point of view. Openness requires careful thought by the practitioner, and encourages reflection on personal responses; an evaluation of the importance of data; and allows for scrutiny by supervisors and other stakeholders.

Emotions

The place of emotions in decision-making and particularly in relation to social work must not be overlooked. It has long been recognised that developing emotional intelligence and being alert to one's own emotional responses and what they might mean in the context of interactions with children and families, is essential to effective practice. That great teacher of social work, Clare Winnicot, wrote powerfully in 1977 about the impact of emotions on social work with children.

> Whenever a social worker intervenes in the life of a family which includes a child or children there is a story behind the intervention, and the social worker needs to know that story and its effect on each child, and to live through the experience with the child as fully as possible, without denying the pain, and accepting the sadness, anger and depression that the situation gives rise to. In this way, moments of great pain can become moments of truth on which a future might be built.

---

1 A mathematical or statistical approach based on interpretations drawn from risk analysis schedules or checklists.

Winnicott (1977) also pointed out the need for awareness within social work departments of the support needed for social workers dealing with emotionally demanding situations, when she wrote:

> Social service departments need to allow for this strain on their social work staff, to understand it, and to devise ways of meeting it within the structure and organisation of the department.

What Winnicott is highlighting is the potential of emotion to help a practitioner's understanding of a situation. For example, a social worker faced for the first time with the expression of grief by a seven-year-old girl at being returned to foster carers at the end of a contact visit with her mother, will need to balance the natural human response of wanting to comfort the child and stem the expression of grief, with the benefits to the child of being able to express their feelings. Working with the child's feelings, rather than against them, is likely to help the worker build their own understanding of the child's inner world and the family relationships and circumstances.

A practitioner who is practised at understanding their own emotional responses will recognise that when they feel depressed or helpless after interviewing a particular client this might give insight into what the client is feeling or experiencing.

O'Sullivan (1999) points out that a wide range of emotions are experienced in social work – fear, anxiety, hope, compassion – and that social workers have to cope with their own emotions and those of the clients and other stakeholders.

A model for understanding the nature of expertise

In her book *Effective Child Protection* (2002), Munro introduces a model (see page 13) to aid understanding of the nature of expertise, or in other words, categories of knowledge and skills that come into play when social workers are making judgements and decisions.

Munro's model was introduced to practitioners during the Putting analysis into assessment project and assisted them in reflecting on their decisions and, in so doing, to become attuned to the usefulness of unpicking and reflecting on decisions and judgements. This was part of the process of developing a critical and reflective mindset.

The model was described to practitioners as being a bit like listening to an orchestra or a band playing. You can either, simply listen and enjoy the music; or you can try and listen for particular instruments and appreciate the role they are playing in the overall sound. Once you have started to do this it tends to stay with you as a way of listening. The practitioners found Munro's 'Pie chart' model helpful as it made them more conscious of the formal knowledge they were drawing on; the critical skills they were using; and how factors such as emotions and experience were coming into play.

Practice tool 1: A model of expertise

Munro's model

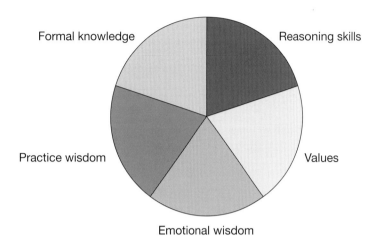

Values: all practice takes place in an ethical framework including, for example, consideration of the balance of rights and needs and awareness of discrimination in all its forms.

Reasoning skills: ability to reflect critically on one's practice; and reason, from a basis of experience and knowledge. Ability to understand the balance between intuition and analysis in one's own decisions; and the ability to make a conscious appraisal of risks and benefits flowing from actions.

Emotional wisdom: awareness of the emotional impact of the work on oneself and others and the ability to deal with this and use it as a source of understanding about behaviour of children, families, self and other professionals.

Practice wisdom: folk psychology, social norms, cultural diversity; a combination of everyday skills and wisdom with enriched skills drawn from training and practice experience.

Formal knowledge: law, policies and procedures and theories; empirical research evidence drawn, for example, from training and reading.

The above model is reproduced and adapted from Munro, E (2002) 'Categories of knowledge and skills', p.12, Figure 2.1.

Case study: A referral

Ellen is on duty in an office in a Midlands town. A referral comes in from the local general hospital antenatal department. Adanna, a 32-year-old Nigerian woman has walked into the accident and emergency department apparently in the early stages of labour. She has not attended any antenatal appointments and is not known to the hospital. She has a three-year-old child with her, a little girl called Ifeoma. Adanna has told the A&E doctors that she is HIV positive but that she does not know if her child Ifeoma is. Adanna is also very poorly with pre-enclampsia, a condition associated with high blood pressure in later pregnancy.

She has given her address as a hotel on Ellen's patch and states that she has lived in the area for three weeks, having moved from London where she had lived with her boyfriend for 18 months. She states that she came to this country two years ago from Nigeria but is unable to say anything about her current status.

The child, Ifeoma, seems well dressed and well fed. Adanna has named her sister as her next of kin and given an address in West London for her.

The hospital are asking Social Services to make arrangements to care for Ifeoma in the short term. Staff also state that there may be other decisions to be made once the baby is born, depending on the outcomes of the tests and how unwell Adanna is.

Ellen will be drawing on knowledge, skills and values drawn from different sections of the pie chart in deciding what actions to take and how to work with this situation.

Formal knowledge will be required because she needs to know the legal framework that sets out the local authority's responsibilities for Ifeoma. She will know that there is a requirement to work in partnership wherever possible with Adanna and enable her to bring up her own child. She will also know that she has to undertake checks with Health and Education and other agencies to find out any relevant information, and that these agencies have a duty to cooperate under Part V of the Children Act 1989. She will have to make a decision whether to receive Ifeoma into care under Section 20 of the Children Act 1989, or indeed whether Ifeoma could be placed with Adanna's sister and receive support as a Child in Need under Section 17 of the 1989 Act. Formal knowledge about child development theory and attachment theory will also affect the decision about where to place Ifeoma. Knowledge of local procedures will determine how Ellen consults with her managers in making the decision. Ellen will also need formal knowledge of asylum and immigration policy and procedures, or will need to take advice from someone who has this knowledge.

Practice wisdom may come into play as Ellen draws on her own past experience of placing children with local foster carers. Her knowledge of the skills and attitudes of local carers may well impact upon the decision. Her knowledge of the likely attitudes and practices within the local hospital will also come into play. Ellen has worked with a number of mothers who are HIV positive, is part of a network of practitioners who work in this area and has undergone a significant amount of training. Ellen's past experience with a similar case, was that, when the Home Office were contacted for information the mother in question went underground. This means that Ellen will wait until she has been able to build some trust with Adanna before taking these steps again.

Emotional wisdom features, as Ellen is able to predict the possible range of Ifeoma's emotional reactions to separation from her mother and is able to discuss with foster carers the meaning of her responses and behaviour. Ellen is herself pregnant and is aware that this particular referral will stir up feelings in her that will possibly be heightened by her experience of pregnancy. Emotional wisdom will also determine the level to which she is able to engage with Ifeoma and her mother.

Values will come into play. Ellen adheres strongly to values about working in partnership, so will do all she can to involve Adanna in the decisions made about Ifeoma and will keep her informed about her progress. She will be aiming to get Ifeoma reunited with Adanna as soon as Adanna is well enough to care for her. She will also work with sensitivity to the cultural differences between herself and Adanna; and Adanna's experiences of living in a society where the dominant culture is different to her own. She feels strongly that parents and children affected by HIV have a right to confidentiality and to retain control over how their medical and social needs are met.

Reasoning skills will come into play when Ellen reflects on how her own assumptions and those of the medical staff – and indeed Adanna and Ifeoma – are affecting their responses to one another and their expectations. Reasoning skills will also operate when Ellen thinks through the consequences of decisions that are going to need to be taken; such as where to place Ifeoma and how to manage contact.

Practice development session 1: The nature of expertise

This session can either be done with a whole team during a team meeting or as part of a longer training course.

Aim

To encourage practitioners to reflect on the range of skills, knowledge and experience that they draw on in practice and to apply this understanding to practice.

Method

- Begin by asking the group what they understand by the word **expertise**. Allow everyone in the group to contribute by means of an **ideas storm**. Write down everything that is said, on a whiteboard or flip chart, without questioning it.

- Generate a discussion about who it is that participants feel have expertise in children and families work; and how different people within the system view it. If necessary, prompt them asking questions such as: Who do parents/teachers/magistrates/social workers/ children tend to view as experts? Why?

- Give a presentation on the nature of expertise; the dichotomy between thinkers (analytical and intuitive); and the importance of both analytical and intuitive thinking over the years using the relevant slides from Presentation 2. Download from www.ncb.org.uk/resources/ support. Stop after the 'Exercise' slide.

- Ask participants to generate a list of the strengths and weaknesses of analytical and intuitive approaches. Then resume the slide show, which will provide feedback on their list.

- Introduce the slide of the pie chart and explain the range of knowledge, skills and so on that a practitioner might be using when making a decision.

- Invite the participants to form pairs. Distribute Munro's model (page 13), one to each pair. You may also want to give them case study: A referral, which illustrates the model used within a case.

- Ask participants, in their pairs, to reflect on their practice over the past couple of months and think about how they have drawn on the various sections of the pie chart. If necessary, prompt them by asking: Do you tend to rely on one part of the pie chart or does it vary depending on the type of case? What external factors impact on how you draw on the sections of the pie chart? Has reflecting on this led you to think that you need to change the way in which you draw on the sections of the pie chart? If so, is there anything you can do about this?

- Reconvene the full group. Invite feedback on the key points from the discussion. If necessary, prompt them by asking: Did this help you to think about the knowledge, skills and experience you are drawing on in your practice? Has it highlighted any of your strengths or weaknesses? Does it have any implications for your individual practice or team's practice? Are there any actions you can use to strengthen your practice, based on the issues that have been highlighted today?

- **Alternatively (or in addition)** ask participants to think through one particular case, remembering key decisions that were made and deciding which elements of the pie chart came into play – this activity to be done as individuals, followed either by discussion in pairs or a general feedback session in the full group. One person could be asked to talk through their case and describe how the different elements were drawn upon at different times. (For further details of this activity, see The Critical decision method on page 124.)

Cultural review

This section introduces the idea of applying approaches more usually used in social research to assist in the assessment situation. In particular we focus on the Cultural review, which is a method of examining cultural assumptions.

In her book *Child and Family Assessment in Social Work Practice* (2004), Holland explores the importance of the impact of the social worker on the assessment relationship and introduces the notion of the reflective and reflexive practitioner. She describes reflexivity as follows.

> *A circular process of thought and action, with our thoughts and beliefs interacting with and affecting service users, and their responses and experiences in turn affecting our thoughts and belief systems.*

Holland refers to the need to be critically aware of the impact of ourselves and our belief systems on the assessment; and of the service users' response to this. She suggests that this will include 'categories' associated with ourselves, such as gender, race and professional status; our agency culture; and dominant theories, practices and assumptions within our occupation. She highlights the need to address these issues in supervision and also, if appropriate, with service users.

She explores some of the literature (Anderson 1990, Farmer and Owen 1995) that looks at the importance of being sensitive to the impact of issues, such as gender and ethnicity, on the allocation of cases.

This is also an area that was explored in Holland's Coastal Cities Study (Holland 2004). In her study, social workers were invited to reflect upon their own contribution to the assessment relationship. They identified some of the difficulties involved, such as power differentials on the grounds of class, race and gender; and were also invited to examine the compensatory tactics they used to minimise the effects of these potential barriers in practice. One social worker interviewed on the study stated the following.

> *I am very much aware that I am a mixed race man and she is a white woman, I think we have some common ground in the fact that we both have small children and I can disclose things about my children and so on ... I think in a sense the issues of class relate to the fact that I am employed, in full-time employment and she isn't, so I mean there's an imbalance there.*

The worker concerned was able to highlight some of the imbalances in the relationship between himself and a client and some of the practices he had used to minimise these.

Holland makes the case for applying methods more usually applied by social researchers – in gathering, organising and analysing data – to the social work task of assessment. Several of her suggestions have been incorporated into this toolkit, including her thoughts on hypothesising and on organising data in reports.

One method introduced in Holland's book (2004), which was originally suggested by McCracken (1988) and featured in Shaw (1997), is called a 'cultural review'.

This is a method for systematically looking at all our cultural categories in relation to the subject at hand. Ideally, it is suggested, this should be carried out at an early stage in the assessment. The purpose of undertaking the cultural review is for the practitioner to alert themselves to areas where their own assumptions, prejudices or simply lack of knowledge might have a bearing on their response to a family and, ultimately, on the approach taken to working with them. Similarly, issues that a worker may be carrying in their head, such as agency norms and awareness, will also have an impact; as will the families' likely assumptions about the worker and the agency.

Perhaps the most appropriate point to undertake a cultural review, time permitting, would be before the first interview or contact with a family after a referral has been received.

The review consists of a series of trigger questions. It is possible to do it as a detailed exercise taking from 20 to 40 minutes; or else, as is much more likely to be practicable, practitioners should, with a bit of practice, be able to hold the questions in their head and address them mentally before a first meeting and then reflect upon the process afterwards.

This model was introduced to practitioners on the Putting analysis into assessment project. The feedback received was that social workers were surprised by some of the answers generated by the exercise. Most of them found it very useful and felt that they would be likely to use it again in practice. One worker commented that it assisted with analysing information, arguing for resources and explaining a decision to a colleague. She also said that:

> Particular needs/requirements were highlighted as were differing world views and methods of interpreting events and conducting life tasks.

This model is applicable to developing a more analytical approach to assessment in that it reveals at an early stage some of the unconscious processes and hidden influences on a practitioner's ability to engage with families. This process is referred to by McCracken (1988, p.33) in Holland (2004, p.130) as 'familiarisation and defamiliarisation', which means that by bringing assumptions and underlying influences on our thinking into awareness we can stand apart from them and see them more objectively and, if necessary, take compensatory action. In Case study: Cultural review, we have shown how two different cases could generate answers in the cultural review. These are drawn from social workers' responses to the cultural review questions during the Putting analysis into assessment project.

Practice tool 2: Cultural review questions

- What do I know about individuals and families with this particular cultural background or life experience?

- Where does my knowledge come from?

- What prejudices may I hold (positive or negative)?

- What do I know/expect about children of this (these) age(s), their lives and needs?

- What might surprise me about this family and why would it be a surprise?

- How might this family/the parents/child/siblings/community perceive me?

- How might the assessment and my agency be perceived?

- What impact might the assessment have on the family's life and on their perception of their lives?

- What agency norms and practices do I take with me on an assessment? (For example, awareness of risk, thresholds of 'good enough parenting', resource restrictions.)

The cultural review questions above, based on McCracken's (1988) *Cultural Review* and featured in Shaw (1997), are based on Holland's (2004, p.130) use of the questions for social work assessment.

Case study: Cultural review exercise

During the Putting analysis into assessment project, a number of groups of participants completed the cultural review exercise. Table below gives examples of the responses given by two different groups after being given very brief details of referrals.

Cultural review questions	Responses from practitioners	
	Case details	*Case details*
	3-month-old baby of Somalian origin	**12- and 14-year-old White British girls**
	Referring agent: Police/ immigration	*Referring agent:* School
	Reason for referral: 17-year-old minor/ asylum seeker with baby – unaccompanied	*Reason for referral:* Concerns re parental discipline, poor attendance, poor hygiene, parental mental health issues
	Family structure: No known family at present	*Family structure:* Mum (29 yrs), Dad (32 yrs), 14 yr old girl, 12 yr old girl, 3 yr old boy, 10 mth old twins, boy and girl
	Other agencies involved: Police, immigration, who have reference to NASS we assume	*Other agencies involved:* School, HV, CPN, school nurse, Connexions, GP, NSPCC (anon. Refs), CPU
	Family previously known? Not to social services locally	*Family previously known?* Parents in care. Also previous sec 17 practical and financial help
	Length of time in area: 12 hours – presumed	*Length of time in area:* 12 months (moved around Midlands)
	Other significant information: Baby sick/dehydrated and malnourished	*Other significant information:* Isolated and stigmatised in local community, don't take up support, housing issues, financial – don't manage well
What do I know about individuals and families with this particular cultural background or life experience?	Nothing/language/ malnutrition– poverty childcare culture/'difficult to work with' (hearsay) large extended family at home	Early pregnancy, poor education, poor employment, low self-esteem/self-worth. MH problems. Attachment problems – also relate to their attachment to their children. Little family support. Distrust of agencies/ dislike of SSD. Fear of childcare support. Aware of 'the system'
Where does my knowledge come from?	Media/other professionals/ previous experience of asylum seekers/lack of knowledge = assumptions	Research/reading/ literature. Practice wisdom, knowledge, colleagues, personal experience, service users, training, and other agencies

Cultural review questions	Responses from practitioners	
	Case details	*Case details*
What prejudices may I hold (positive or negative)?	As above/presume needs resources and help and assume entrance is illegal	Failure to parent, history 'repeating itself'. As above, mostly negative
What do I know/expect about children of this (these) age(s), their lives and needs?	Good experience of child development – realistic expectations, very dependent, needs complete care. Needs strong attachment to care giver	Time of change, identity quite well established in behaviour. Guarded and protective of family. May be young carers. Friends/peers important. May be rebellious. Emotional problems/moody. Peer pressure. Expectations from school – academic pressure. Poor supervision at home. Need a lot of feeding. Self-image – fashion
What might surprise me about this family and why would it be a surprise?	If came in legally to meet up with family/ if doesn't want support/ if has financial support/if can speak English fluently/ to meet up with wealthy family	Strengths and resilience can be challenging to professionals. Prejudices regarding passivity and 'client'
How might this family/the parents/child/siblings/ community, perceive me?	Official/threatening/ powerful/take child?/ judging	**Parents:** Threat, unrealistic, interfering, helpful, understanding, bit of a pushover **Children (12 & 14):** fearful – 'care', helpful, willing to listen to them, concerned, make it worse/better
How might the assessment and my agency be perceived?	As above	Unnecessary, interfering provider of services/goods/items, unpredictable, frightening
What impact might the assessment have on the family's life and on their perception of their lives?	Major – might have to return/undermine parenting/self-esteem/ values	Might give some insight. Provide some resources, help with parenting, improve. Might have little effect
What agency norms and practices do I take with me on an assessment? (For example, awareness of risk, thresholds of 'good enough parenting', resource restrictions)	Financial resources/ timescales/risk of significant harm/thresholds/ individual perceptions of agency's 'norms'/procedures and other agencies' procedures	ACPC – guidance and procedures on neglect. Thresholds for assessment. Lack of intensive family support resources locally. 'Heartsink' case – not much we can do – too entrenched

Practice development session 2: Cultural review

Aim

To demonstrate how undertaking a cultural review at the very beginning of a case creates opportunity for openness and reflection about influences on practice.

Method

- Invite participants to form pairs and to ideas storm what they think are the things (assumptions, questions, expectations and baggage) that they might bring to an assessment before they even meet the family. Either ask them to write their ideas down on sticky notes or take feedback from the whole group and record it on a whiteboard or flip chart.

- Reconvene the full group. Give information on cultural review and how it is used by social researchers to help them understand how their own prejudices and experiences might slant the way in which they approach a piece of research, so that they can actively take steps to counter this tendency. Use Presentation 3, slides 23 and 24, or make presentation into a handout and talk through key points (see Appendix or download the presentation from www.ncb.org.uk/resources/support).

- Divide participants into small groups and give them some very brief referral information on a case or on several different cases. (This could be taken from the referral and cultural review Case studies or, if a whole team is present, use cases recently referred to the team.) Distribute the cultural review questionnaire (page 19) and ask the participants to consider the questions in their groups and note down all their responses, even if they vary. Encourage them to discuss and debate but stress that they do not need to reach a consensus.

- Invite feedback from the group – this can be detailed if you have time or just a point from each group.

- Reconvene the full group and ask participants if the activity raised any issues for them. Did they find it helpful? Would it be possible to do this before conducting an assessment? Could they take something useful from it into practice? If time would not allow them to do a full cultural review, could they do an abbreviated version or keep certain questions in their heads to think about whilst on their way to a visit?

It is likely that the exercise has made people think about the prejudices that they and families might hold; and about how cultural issues in wider society and in their own agencies will impact on the way in which they approach a first meeting with a family.

Planning and hypothesising

This section explores the importance of planning and hypothesising in the assessment process. Some planning questions are outlined, followed by an exploration of the meaning and function of hypothesis and its role in supporting open-minded yet critical thinking.

Planning

Most people would agree that one should not set out on any important endeavour without preparing and planning, but we can all think of occasions when time constraints, lack of information and even the triumph of hope over experience meant that we have done just that. Sometimes if we've been lucky things have worked out but if we reflect, honestly, on such occasions, we would probably agree that a better plan would have led to a better outcome. Sue Kerr, a business consultant, is quoted as saying 'Hope is not a plan' and the late Sir John Harvey Jones, the industrialist and television troubleshooter, sums up the temptations of not planning in rather a tongue in cheek fashion:

> Planning is an unnatural process; it is much more fun to do something. The nicest thing about not planning is that failure comes as a complete surprise, rather than being proceeded by a period of worry and depression.

This paints a humorous picture of the hapless fool stumbling towards disaster in blissful ignorance. We are not suggesting that social workers are hapless or foolish, but clearly when the life experiences and possible future life chances of children are at stake, practitioners have a huge responsibility to ensure that they optimise the chances of an assessment leading to a positive outcome for a child. Some may argue that the frameworks and timescales in operation around assessment, in themselves create a kind of plan and clearly the domains and dimensions of The Assessment Framework do contribute towards planning, but there are other practical and practice-focused issues that need to be considered, discussed and reflected upon in order to ensure that the limited amount of time available is used to its best effect and that the assessment is carried out in a coherent, open and fair way.

The Stepwise model of assessment, on page 26, shows planning as the first step in the assessment process, followed by hypothesising. In reality, as explained later in this section, a natural and intuitive response would be to start hypothesising as soon as referral information is received. Nevertheless the model is useful for illustrating the stages that must be completed in order to ensure thoroughness in the process.

The first questions in terms of planning any assessment must focus on the children's immediate safety. For example:

- Are the children safe now?
- Have they experienced or are they at immediate risk of significant harm?
- Is there a need for immediate action to protect them or remove them to a safe place?

In many cases these questions will already have been answered and the necessary action taken prior to commencement of the assessment, but these decisions will need to be continuously reviewed as part of the assessment process.

Other relevant planning questions will be practical and practice focused.

Practical considerations

- Is there clarity and agreement about the type and purpose of assessment required and how frameworks and timescales impact on the plan?
- Who is requesting the assessment and what are their current concerns? Are their goals and expectations understood?
- Who needs to be involved in the assessment – family members, professionals, experts?
- Have the family had previous assessments or contact with agencies?
- Are there any communication issues or considerations such as language, religion, culture, disability and is an interpreter required?
- Who will take what role in the assessment process?
- Who will be lead professional?
- Are the family aware of and in agreement with the need for assessment?
- Where and in what order will the child and other family members be interviewed? Is it possible to plan interviews with children and key family members at an early stage (with their agreement)?
- Is access available to all the formal information that is required for the assessment (past files, information from prior local authorities, chronologies, reports)?
- Are other types of assessment concurrent? If so how will the assessments be linked or integrated?
- Are there sufficient resources, time, personnel, funds, supervision, and specialist expertise available for the assessment to be carried out?
- How much of the time available needs to be allocated to the different activities (interviews, liaising writing up, and so on)?
- Are there any practical or time constraints that limit what can be done in the assessment period?
- What needs to be prioritised and why?

Practice-focused questions

- What are the questions that need answering through the assessment, what are the issues and what are the likely consequences for the child's health and development of the present situation?
- Is there agreement across the professional network about the current concerns and issues that the assessment must address?
- Are there any anticipated barriers or personal challenges in carrying out this assessment?
- Is the worker competent to carry out this assessment? Do they possess the necessary knowledge, skills and experience and if not how will this be addressed in the plan?
- What are the parameters to this type of assessment and what is the range and limitations of possible outcomes? Has this been acknowledged with children, parents, family members and other professionals?
- What are the unconscious processes at work in this situation that may impact on the interaction between family and practitioner? (See the Cultural review questions on pages 20–1).
- How might the child and family's involvement in the assessment be supported and encouraged?
- What support and guidance does the practitioner require?

Addressing the questions above will help in the formulation of a plan and will contribute to reflective practice. No plan is perfect and revision will almost certainly be necessary during the course of the assessment but it is far better to have a plan from which to digress, and be able to justify this, than to work in an unplanned and therefore less robust manner.

As mentioned earlier planning and hypothesising are intertwined to some extent in the assessment and it is not always easy to say that one comes before the other but both are critical to a full and balanced exploration of the child and family experience.

Hypothesising

The word *hypothesis* has its origins in ancient Greek and means 'a proposition made as a basis for reasoning' (OED). In modern day usage, a hypothesis is a provisional idea or explanation which has to be evaluated or tested. The idea needs to be either confirmed or disproved. The hypothesis should be 'falsifiable', which means it is possible for it to be shown to be false, usually by observation. Even if confirmed, the hypothesis is not necessarily proven, but remains provisional.

Hypothesising is a core activity within social work assessment. Holland (2004) states:

The cornerstone of analysis in assessment work might be seen as the process of building hypotheses for understanding a family situation and developing these until they include a plan for the way forward.

This process of building, testing out and discarding hypotheses starts at the earliest point of contact. As soon as a referral is received into a social work team the practitioner will begin consciously or unconsciously to form some hypotheses of what is happening within the family.

For example, if a headteacher rings the duty team at 5pm to say that they are concerned about a seven-year-old girl who has not been collected from school that day (and who is often not collected on time, regularly arrives at school very late, is often brought by strangers, is usually dirty, unkempt and seemingly underfed), the duty officer is likely to be mentally hypothesising about what is happening within the family during the initial conversation. They may have several hypotheses that spring to mind immediately, of which the following are an example.

1. Parent has started working and has not been able to arrange proper childcare for child.

2. Parent or carer is depressed or ill and has become unable to meet the child's day-to-day needs.

3. Child is a scapegoat within the family and is therefore neglected or abused.

4. This is a chaotic family who only just cope at the best of times and some event has occurred to tip them into an unacceptable level of chaotic neglect.

5. The child's parents are misusing alcohol or other substances and are often too 'out of it' and unable to care properly for the child or bring her to school.

They would certainly check out some of their hypotheses during an initial conversation with the referrer and may even ditch one or more of them at this stage. The formation of various hypotheses and the decision taken about the steps needed to investigate the matter further will be influenced by a range of factors, for example: practice wisdom, personal values, and formal knowledge.

The practitioner is also likely to be susceptible to what Sheldon (1987) and Scott (1998) (cited in Holland 2004) refer to as 'our natural human tendency to be "verificationists"'. This means that we tend to form an explanation for a family's or individual's circumstances early on in our contact with them and then we tend to seek information that will confirm these original hypotheses.

Similarly, Munro's research (1999) into the findings of inquiries into child deaths highlights that a common error identified in inquiries was a 'failure to revise risk assessments' and that in numerous cases there was failure to check more widely or reappraise original judgements when new evidence arose.

Hollows (2003) refers to this tendency as 'unconflicted adherence', that is, where a new risk is discounted and the current strategy is maintained without change.

Raynes in Calder and others (2003) suggests that workers often remain narrowly focused on proving or disproving whether the original risk remains and fail to consider the broader picture. He suggests that practitioners should consider all the possibilities about what is happening and address each hypothesis, only discarding it when there is clear evidence to do so. In the Stepwise approach to assessment, as shown in the illustration below, the hypothesis stage first appears early in the process of assessment. Although one would argue that, as demonstrated earlier, the process of hypothesising starts earlier, that is, at the point of referral, this model is nevertheless helpful for giving a structured approach to the stages of the assessment process and the place of forming, testing out and discarding hypotheses within that process.

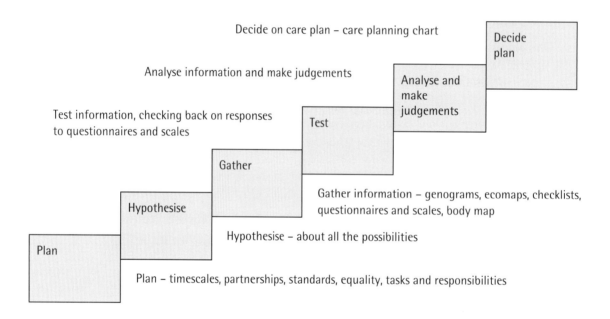

Illustration of hypothesis within the stepwise model of assessment

The above model is based on work by De Mello and Yuille and is adapted from Calder and Hacket (2003) *Assessment in Childcare: Using and developing frameworks for practice*, p.122, Figure 1 'A stepwise model for children and family assessments'.

The illustration above locates the various assessment activities at the specific stages of the stepwise model. Similarly, Margaret Adcock (2000) describes several overlapping phases of assessment and further explores the distinctions between analysis, judgements and decisions.

As identified earlier, the process of hypothesising might continue throughout the assessment process as long as new information continues to emerge. The information should be drawn from a range of sources using a variety of methods. In order to counter the verificationist tendency earlier identified, Holland (2004) argues as follows.

We should always look for data, or information, that might disprove, or at least throw doubt on, our understanding. The reason for such an orientation is that it actively works against our human tendency to distort what we see in order to fit with our fixed explanations.

New information is sought with the specific purpose of increasing understanding about what is happening within the family and how this is impacting on the well-being of the child or children under consideration. It is vital to make the search wide-ranging and to do it in partnership with family members as much as possible. Using different strategies for gathering the information, rather than relying on one narrow method, is also important. Methods for gathering information may include the following.

1. Interviewing parents and children

2. Interviewing professionals who know the family

3. Employing direct observation and child observation

4. Using questionnaires and scales with family members

5. Using play or drawing and creative approaches to communicating with children

6. Making reference to research or theory

Testing and evaluating hypotheses is a key part of the process. The timescales ascribed to different levels of assessment (initial and core) will limit the depth of exploration that can be undertaken but, even in an initial assessment, it is possible and indeed expected to generate possible hypotheses and explore these. Indeed, noting that some important hypotheses have not been tested during an initial assessment may well indicate that a core assessment is necessary in order to undertake further enquiries.

Practice tool 3: Questions to assist in developing and testing hypotheses

What different hypotheses exist about this situation? Try to think widely and develop a number even if you can discount them quicky				
What are different hypotheses based on? For example, observation, reports, the evidence base, theory, assumptions				
What methods will you use to test out, disconfirm or substantiate the hypotheses? Remember that a variety of methods will be needed to avoid a narrow focus				
When tested, do the hypotheses stand up or have they been discounted? Remember to be rigorous and not favour evidence that supports your original idea				
Have any new hypotheses emerged during the assessment process? If so give details here				
What further actions need to be taken to disconfirm or substantiate new or existing hypotheses?				
What conclusions can be drawn in relation to the different hypotheses? And what does this indicate for the recommendations of the assessment?				

Case study: Hypothesising

Name	Age	Gender	Ethnicity	Status/relationship
Tricia Gibbons	34	female	White British	mother
Miklovan Murati	34	male	Albanian	Anna's father
Anna Murati	7 months	female	dual-heritage Albanian/English	daughter of Tricia & Miklovan
Frankie Johnson	6	male	dual-heritage (African-Caribbean/White British)	son of Tricia & Ashleigh
Nathan Johnson	8	male	dual-heritage (same as Frankie)	son of Tricia & Ashleigh
Natalie Graves	15	female	White British	daughter of Tricia & Steve Graves
Ashleigh Johnson	32	male	African-Caribbean	Nathan and Frankie's father
Steve Graves	38	male	White British	Natalie's father

Tricia is a 34-year-old woman who lives with her partner and her four children in Sandley, a metropolitan borough in the West Midlands. The family moved into the borough from a neighbouring one about eight months ago, just before the birth of Anna.

Miklovan is the father of the youngest child, Anna. He is Albanian and, as far as the professionals are aware, Miklovan was previously an asylum seeker. However, further details around his current immigration status are unknown to the professionals. He has lived with Tricia for the last two years.

The father of Frankie and Nathan is Tricia's ex-husband, Ashleigh, who now lives in Birmingham. He has some contact with the boys. This usually occurs when he rings and arranges to pick up the boys to take them over to Birmingham for the weekend or during the school holidays. The arrangement is a loose one with no particular pattern to it.

Natalie's father, Tricia's first husband Steve, is serving a twelve-year prison sentence for armed robbery. He has not lived with Tricia since Natalie was two years old, although he was having regular monthly contact with Natalie until he went to prison last year.

Anna's father Miklovan has been living with the family for eighteen months but his current whereabouts are unclear.

The referral

The referral has been made by the health visitor because of concerns about Anna's development. She is underweight and has dropped below the 25th centile (she was at the 50th centile at her previous check). She was growing well for the first three months, but her progress has slowed in the last four. A referral has been made to the child development clinic for developmental tests to try to establish if there is any organic cause for the developmental slowdown.

Tricia maintains that Anna is feeding well, but the health visitor is concerned because the house is in a filthy state after having been reasonably tidy and clean initially when she started visiting. Anna is often wearing a heavily soiled nappy when the health visitor visits. Tricia has become withdrawn and uncommunicative, possibly depressed. The health visitor has observed a lack of affection and engagement with Anna, although she has observed Natalie picking her up and playing with her when she has been there. Tricia does not seem to be particularly responsive to the health visitor's concerns about Anna's development.

The health visitor is not sure if Miklovan is still living with the family and says Tricia is evasive when asked. The health visitor hasn't seen him there for some time.

Checks with school reveal that they had been on the verge of making a referral to social services because of a build-up of recent concerns connected with the boys. Frankie is well behind the expected attainment levels for his age; he finds it difficult to cope in the classroom setting and seems very angry, often fighting with other children. Nathan is more settled and doing okay, but both boys often turn up late and are collected late. They have a lot of time off and they are often grubby and unkempt. Frankie recently commented to a classroom assistant that his mum was upset because Miklovan had 'gone off on one again' and had 'smashed Nathan's PlayStation and gone to Bolton'.

Natalie is in Year 11 at secondary school, her GCSE year, but has had a lot of absences recently, which have caused concern in relation to her forthcoming exams, and coursework completion deadlines. Otherwise, the school sees her as a quiet, unassuming girl. Parents have not attended open evenings and phone calls home have had little response.

Examples of the different hypotheses generated and plans for testing them out*

Hypotheses	Methods for testing hypotheses
Domestic violence	Ask Tricia, Physical evidence, Talk to children, Speak to domestic violence team, Speak to other agencies, Investigate previous relationships, Talk to extended family, Use Fahlberg scale
Miklovan has a positive influence on the family. Things have deteriorated recently since he left	Ask Tricia, Talk to children, Make visits at different times of day, Make unannounced visits, Talk to schools, Clarify with health visitor
Tricia is depressed (post-natal depression?)	Use HV Edinburgh questionnaire, Check post-natal depression score, Use Adult Wellbeing Scale (DH and others 2000), Ask Tricia how she feels, Use observation, Liaise with other agencies, Talk to children, Talk to health visitor
Financial difficulties/impact of poverty	Talk to Tricia, Look at financial information/examine benefits take-up, etc.
On the run from CP registration in another authority; or Miklovan's unknown whereabouts linked to uncertain immigration status	Checks with other agencies and other authorities
Organic cause of failure to thrive	Check HV records, Refer to child development clinic
Socially excluded family, therefore more vulnerable	Talk to Tricia, Talk to children, Explore networks of support, such as neighbours' groups
Physical abuse of children esp. Frankie and Nathan by Miklovan	Look for physical evidence, Examine agency checks for previous incidents, Talk to Frankie and Nathan
Natalie is a young carer	Talk to Natalie on her own, Talk to Natalie with Tricia, Explain 'young carer' definitions and introduce local services

* These hypotheses and plans to carry them out were developed by groups participating in a practice development exercise, based on Case study: Cultural review, during the Putting analysis into assessment project.

As with the previous activity, the above are simply examples of answers generated during the practice development exercise with participants on the Putting analysis into assessment project. They are not right or wrong. The intention is to maintain a needs-based approach to making enquires and, by keeping the possible hypotheses in mind when planning enquiries, there is perhaps more likelihood of asking questions and talking to people who may provide greater insight into the circumstances of the different family members through a variety of routes.

Practice development session 3: Hypothesising

Aim

To help practitioners understand the meaning of hypothesising during assessment and to test this out in practice.

Method

- Begin **either** by asking participants what they understand by the word *hypothesis*.

- **Or** invite participants to form pairs to discuss hypothesising. Tell them to prepare answers, to be shared with the full group, to questions such as: What is hypothesising? When should it happen? Who should be involved?

- Whether the task was performed by the participants in pairs or otherwise, invite participants to share their answers. Record the answers, without questioning them, on a flip chart.

- Explain to the participants what hypothesising is (using notes on hypothesising from this section; or the relevant slides from Presentation 3. Download from www.ncb.org.uk/resources/support).

- Distribute Case study: Hypothesising or a case study of your own choosing, or, if a team is participating in the course, one drawn from one of the team's real cases.

- Organise the participants into groups of four and distribute the Practice Tool 3 to assist in developing and testing hypotheses. Ask the groups to generate as many possible hypotheses as they can in the time allowed (around 15 minutes). Invite feedback from the groups, taking one hypothesis from each group and logging all of the on the flip sheet until all of the hypotheses that the groups developed have been recorded. Discuss how the different hypotheses would be tested out and how one activity, for example interviewing Natalie, could help to test out several different hypotheses. Emphasise the point about needing to keep all hypotheses alive throughout the assessment and to test them until there is information that would enable them to discard or confirm them.

- Reconvene the full group. Invite each small group to take one hypothesis. Using Practice Tool 3 work through one line from top to bottom completing the first three boxes on the left. Discuss the issues that might come up, how the issues would have an impact on the completion of the next four boxes and how participants would deal with this. Encourage discussion on how to incorporate this approach into the timescales of initial and core assessments. Ask whether they foresee any difficulties and how they might overcome them. Record all the positive actions suggested for overcoming the potential difficulties.

3. Conducting the assessment

Needs analysis

This section deals with the importance of taking a needs-led approach to assessment. Furthermore, it looks at how taking a holistic approach to the needs of children from the outset of assessment, assists with analysis throughout the process and contributes to better outcomes for children.

Practitioners are, on the whole, conversant with the basic principles of taking a needs-led approach to assessment. This section, however, offers an opportunity to focus on needs with practitioners to provide them with both a timely reminder and an opportunity to step back and consider how needs-led their own practice and the culture of their team and agency actually are.

As mentioned in the Introduction, *The Framework for the Assessment of Children in Need and Their Families* (Department of Health and others 2000) was intended to provide a systematic way of analysing, understanding and recording what is happening to children and young people – both within their families and in the wider context of the community in which they live – in order to be able to make professional judgements about them. These judgements include whether the child is in need or suffering significant harm; what actions must be taken; and what services would best meet the needs of that particular child and family.

Part III of The Children Act 1989 lays out the duty on local authorities to provide services to safeguard and promote the welfare of children in need and provides a definition of a child in need, deeming that a child is in need if:

a)   he is unlikely to achieve or maintain or to have the opportunity of achieving or maintaining a reasonable standard of health or development without the provision for him of services by a local authority or

b)   his health and development is likely to be significantly impaired or further impaired without the provision for him of such services or

c)   he is disabled.

The Children Act 1989 set out a framework within which children in need and their families would be provided with services in order to ensure the child achieved his or her expected developmental outcomes. Research studies, commissioned by the Department of Health on the working of the child protection system in England and Wales and published in *Child Protection: Messages from research* in 1995, showed that child protection concerns continued to be the main trigger by which families gained access to services.

In many authorities it was only if there was evidence of potential significant harm that access to family support services could be gained, which was directly against the intentions of Part III of the Act. The absence of a consistent approach to the assessment of children in need meant that similar children were being treated very differently in different authorities.

The Assessment Framework was introduced as part of the government's broad aim of improving outcomes for children in need and, in particular, to support the objective for children's social services in 1999: *to ensure that referral and assessment processes discriminate effectively between different types and levels of need and produce a timely service response* (DH and others 2000).

The Assessment Framework takes the broad approach to identifying children in need that the Children Act 1989 intended. It is a conceptual map to gather and analyse information about children and families, in order to determine if a child is in need and what services are required to address those needs. It is informed by extensive research and practice knowledge and is based on the following principles, that is, that assessments should be:

- child-centred

- rooted in child development

- designed to ensure equality of opportunity

- ecological in their approach

- carry an assumption of close inter-agency working

- viewed as a continuing process

- carried out in parallel with other actions, including the provision of services.

Needs and rights

As mentioned earlier, the developments in policy and processes in children's services have taken place within the wider context of a growing understanding of service user rights and participation, but balancing children's needs and rights can be challenging. Are they always the same thing and how can we ensure that rights have been fully addressed when constructing plans for children?

The United Nations Convention the Rights of the Child provides an essential framework for practice. Munro (2011) refers to the UNCRC as the manifestation of the recognition of the importance of children's safety and welfare. Nelson Mandela described it as:

> *that luminous living document that enshrines the rights of every child without exception to a life of dignity and self fulfillment.*
>
> *(Listen and Change – Participation Works 2008)*

The UNCRC, developed between 1979 and 1989 by the international community and adopted in the UK in 1989 includes over 40 substantive rights for children, including economic, social, cultural and political rights, and it emphasisises the importance of prioritising the child's best interests, full protection from all forms of violence and the right to education that helps children develop as fully as possible. Article 12 of the UNCRC, the most widely quoted article in discussion of children's rights and participation, assures the right for children who are capable of forming his or her own views the right to express those views feely in all matters affecting them and that those views be given due weight in accordance with the age and maturity of the child.

However, the translation of a rights-based approach into everyday practice has been a major challenge. This has not been helped by a lack of human rights information and training across the public and voluntary sector and more generally a poor understanding, engagement and prioritising of human rights in public life. Evidence from training sessions shows that many practitioners can often only demonstrate a very limited understanding of UNCRC and its relevance to assessment practice and successive governments have been challenged about the depth of their commitment to the UNCRC (Guardian online 4.10.2008).

So how would a greater focus on children's rights improve the analysis of their needs? While not wishing to oversimplify the complexities involved, at the very least it should ensure that an exploration of needs and how well they are being met within the family remains firmly focused on the child's experience, their perceptions and descriptions (where possible) of that experience and it should mean that the child becomes an active agent in the process, rather than passive recipient of attention.

Indeed, the first principle of an effective child protection system described by Munro (2011) is one where:

> everyone involved in child protection should pursue child-centred working and
> recognise children and young people as individuals with rights, including their right
> to participation in decisions about them in line with their age and maturity.

Involving children is covered in more detail later in this chapter, but here the focus is on how a detailed understanding of needs can help to keep the child firmly at the centre of the process and prevent the tendency to rush to conclusions too quickly or recommend interventions and services without a detailed appraisal of how they might help.

Needs versus risks?

Some have argued that the emphasis on children's needs in the Assessment Framework dangerously ignores risk to children, and specifically the risk of significant harm (Calder and others 2004). However, focusing only on risks has severe limitations.

There had been something of a preoccupation, over the twenty years or so prior to the development of the Assessment Framework, with models for risk assessment that tended to stress family dysfunction rather than strengths (Seden and others 2001). This is in some part explained by the public and professional anxiety response resulting from highly publicised child-death inquiries; and a desire to be able to predict the risks to children's welfare associated with 'parental dangerousness'. Risk assessment schedules offer a range of predictors and factors derived from what, in the past, have contributed to dangerous actions. They provide a map of clusters of factors which, when aggregated, indicate cause for concern (Seden and others 2001).

A number of commentators have, however, drawn attention to the problems thrown up by over-reliance on such materials. There are reasons to be cautious about their use. Literature from the United States has identified problems of inadequate implementation, evaluation, and difficulties of working with complex and variable data.

Social workers are involved in a balancing act when seeking to protect children, constantly sifting and analysing complex information throughout the assessment to try and identify children's needs and the nature and level of risks posed; indeed this is often a source of tension in their relationships with families and with other professionals as a result of differing perceptions and thresholds of need and risk. Commentators who are most removed from the realities of this process are most likely to be overoptimistic about the possibility of certainty in predicting risk. Munro (2011) refers to:

> the sometimes limited understanding amongst the public and policy makers of the
> unavoidable degree of uncertainty involved in making child protection decisions, and
> the impossibility of eradicating that uncertainty.

Over-reliance on risk assessment instruments that have been developed to help practitioners decide on levels of risk has been shown to be problematic (Munro 2002). Risk assessment instruments developed within one population may have little relevance when transported to another and it is dangerous to apply tools and schedules without due regard to the individual characteristics of the child and family concerned. Wald and Woolverton (1990, p.505 in Cash 2001) said: *In the hands of unskilled workers these instruments may actually produce worse decisions.*

Reporting on a systematic review of studies of outcomes following identification of abuse or neglect, in order to assess the likelihood of a repeat of abuse or other poor outcomes, Jones and others (2006) highlight some of the possible factors that may increase risks of abuse to a child. However they state ultimately that, although these factors might be applied to practice, they cannot be done so *in a precise or numerical way.* They go on to highlight the limitations of numerical and actuarial approaches and offer the following comment.

> *It is highly unlikely that the actuarial approach will take us further than the realm of guidance for a practitioner's individual decision-making simply because of the complex and multi-factorial nature of individual cases in the real world.*

Instead, the authors urge openness as an approach so as to allow for reflection and external scrutiny.

Munro (2002) argues for a standards-based approach, which emphasises transparency of decision-making.

> *Not that they [decisions] are infallible but that they can be shown to be reasonable estimates based on the evidence that was available at the time.*

In short, there is a place for checklists and schedules as helpful mapping tools but they cannot be used without professional judgement. Cash (2001), in an analysis of research about risk-assessment instruments, says that risk-assessment instruments are not a panacea for decision-making in child welfare. He states that decisions should optimally be made through a combination of both empirical evidence [science] and practice wisdom [art], as one without the other is incomplete. He also suggests that the synergy of art and science allows for a more holistic and effective assessment.

Turney and others (2011) in a government research brief, reported that a high quality assessment carried out by competent professionals contributes to better outcomes for children and that an absence of assessment or poor quality assessment from initial assessment right through to decision making in key areas could be shown to have an impact on the likelihood of repeat abuse.

This toolkit stresses that a holistic assessment of needs, using all three domains of the framework, allows for a comprehensive and holistic exploration of those factors that potentially promote or compromise the welfare and safety of the child or children being assessed; and takes into account contextual effects within the family and community systems.

A needs-led approach

A realistic approach to balancing needs and risks of harm is one that adheres to the principles outlined above and combines this with a thorough analysis of the information gathered.

Research by Sinclair (2001, in Seden and others 2001) on the language of need, attempted to identify the language actually used by practitioners to describe the needs of children they were working with to see if patterns and groupings emerged.

This work, commissioned by the Department of Health to inform the development of the Assessment Framework, found that social workers on the whole had little difficulty in applying a needs-focused analysis to their cases. They tended to use language (see examples in italics) that focused on the following aspects (shown in bold text).

- **The causes:** *the break-up of the family and the rejection by both parents; having been sexually abused, she's extra vulnerable.*

- **Manifestation:** *she was self-harming, she was liable to cause herself some sort of permanent damage.*

- **Symptomology:** *he has all these needs about his behaviours but all of these were based on his emotional difficulties, his sense of self.*

And they were described in one of the following ways (shown in bold).

- **Developmental terms:** *developmentally there were issues of neglect ... of weight loss.*

- **Context or circumstances** within which the child was living: *he lives with a single-parent mother who finds it difficult to cope with aspects of his behaviour.*

The research highlighted the multiplicity, complexity and compounding nature of the needs of the children referred to; and the fact that multiplicity of needs may be as important as severity of need. This research again highlights the importance of taking a holistic approach – an approach that is not limited to looking at only one aspect of a child's life experience.

Several years after the implementation of the Assessment Framework, research by Cleaver and Walker (2004) on its implementation suggests that there are ongoing concerns about the ability of practitioners to analyse needs during the assessment process. It also suggests that, whilst most managers identified an improvement in assessments within their agencies as a result of the framework, *a considerable proportion of social workers expressed anxiety about their ability to carry out assessments, particularly how to analyse the information they collected during the assessment and collaborative working with colleagues from other agencies.*

The assessment triangle is now widely understood as the model that identifies the holistic needs of a child in the three different domains: developmental needs; parent's capacity to meet those needs; and the family and environmental context in which the child is living. But time pressures, agency policy and pressures from referrers all contribute to a tendency to slot children and families into existing services, rather than to take the time to make a proper analysis of the needs of a child or children in a family and to decide what interventions or services are most likely to meet those needs.

Throughout the Putting analysis into assessment project, and in numerous training sessions since, an activity focusing on analysis of needs has been included. Despite initial concerns that practitioners would object to being taught how to 'suck eggs', for the most part practitioners and managers welcome an opportunity to reflect together on the degree to which the concept of need remains at the heart of the assessment process. The activity is described in detail in the Needs analysis practice development session (page 43).

Practice tool 4, on page 39, was developed by the authors from materials designed for the National Children's Bureau Care Planning project (Williams and McCann 2006). The idea is to use a staged process for reflection in practice: to identify needs and the reasons why they are unmet or a priority for concern; to consider the negative consequences of them not being met; the long-term outcomes hoped for by meeting the need; and perhaps some staged objectives along the way, prior to deciding what action, intervention or service might best meet that need.

Practitioners have frequently fed back that despite the challenges of reflection in practice it can be helpful to consciously slow the process down so as to ensure that they are able to keep the focus on the child and provide greater clarity about the purpose of interventions and services and the outcomes they are seeking. This more thoughtful approach helps to prevent the 'short circuit' or 'quick fix' described in the CWDC NQSW Supervision handbook (chapter 3 page 18), which happens when practitioners jump from the experiencing stage of Kolb's learning cycle, past the reflection and analysis stages straight to making plans, the outcome of which is that the problem is likely to reoccur. Although when running the exercise we have noted an encouraging shift towards a less service led and more needs led response we still find that some participants find it hard to differentiate between needs and services until the difference is highlighted.

The two case studies (page 40), Sammy and Danny, can be used with practitioners in training or as a practice development session as described on page 43, to help practitioners to identify needs as opposed to services or inputs. They can be substituted with different case scenarios, more relevant to the area of practice, or the characteristics of children worked with.

Practice tool 4: Needs and outcomes form

Needs	Contributory factors	Consequences	Outcomes	Interventions
Identify the child's specific needs under the developmental dimensions from the Framework for Assessment, including needs identified by the child or others.	Why is this need a priority – is this related to a parental capacity issue, or change in family circumstances for example?	What will be the consequence in relation to this need if nothing changes? (negative outcome)	What will be the outcome if the need is met? Think medium and long term and use SMART objectives.	Lastly, what actions, interventions or services are required for this need to be met?
Health				
Education				
Emotional and behavioural development				
Identity				
Family and social relationships				
Social presentation				
Self-care skills				

Case study: Danny

Danny is three. His mother misuses alcohol but her care of her children seemed just about adequate until she met a new partner. He also drank heavily and was violent. There was a drunken fight between Danny's mother and her partner in a local pub and Danny's mother sustained a head injury and was taken to hospital.

Police were involved and found Danny and his seven-year-old sister, Marie, at home on their own. They were grubby and miserable and the police took them into police protection. They have been placed with a local foster carer who says that Marie is worried about her mum and keeps trying to take charge of Danny. Danny is reported to be small for his age and his speech is delayed. He seems to look to Marie for care and affection. He is not toilet-trained and keeps asking where his mummy is.

Danny's needs are ...

Case study: Sammy

Sammy is five and the only child of a mother with schizophrenia. She is devoted to Sammy and cares for him well as long as she takes her medication. Sammy has just started school and the school says that, despite appearing chatty and polite, they feel he is an anxious child. He finds it hard to play with other children and is clingy with the teachers. He says he sleeps in his mum's bed because of the ghosts in the house. She has started turning up during the school day to check he is okay.

Sammy's needs are ...

In the following table, the right-hand column shows some of the responses given during practice development and training sessions. We have found that whilst participants are relatively needs-focused, there is variation in different groups as to the number of examples given of services or interventions as opposed to needs. The responses in italics are the ones that were more service- or input-focused and those not in italics are those that in our view better describe the actual needs of the children.

Case study: Danny	Danny is three. His mother misuses alcohol but her care of her children seemed just about adequate until she met a new partner. He also drank heavily and was violent. There was a drunken fight between Danny's mother and her partner in a local pub and Danny's mother sustained a head injury and was taken to hospital. Police were involved and found Danny and his seven-year-old sister, Marie, at home on their own. They were grubby and miserable and the police took them into police protection. They have been placed with a local foster carer who says that Marie is worried about her mum and keeps trying to take charge of Danny. Danny is reported to be small for his age and his speech is delayed. He seems to look to Marie for care and affection. He is not toilet-trained and keeps asking where his mummy is. Danny's needs are ...	**Health** Good physical care *To live in safe, clean and dry environment* *To receive adequate nutrition* *To be protected from and not be exposed to violence* *Health check/assessment* *Good paediatric assessment* *Assessment of health needs* *LAC Health assessment* *Developmental check* *Health visitor* High standard of physical and emotional care [foster carers] **Education** Needs stimulation Stimulation and socialisation Needs help understanding the situation *Assessment of his mother's ability to change and provide safe care* *Speech therapy* **Emotional and behavioural development** Emotional warmth and attachment Consistent stimulating environment to help develop age-appropriate skills Help to feel safe *Developmental assessment* **Identity** To know about his origins and extended family *Exploration of extended family* **Family and social relationships** Needs a sense of family ... belonging to someone somewhere Appropriate relationship with sister Marie Contact with mother and other significant family members Consistent parenting *Work with mother and stepfather on parenting skills* *Make links with extended family and establish if they can care for him – kinship assessment* *Explicit contract with carer re day to day work with the child* **Social presentation** *Speech therapy* **Self-care skills** *Toilet training*

| Case study: Sammy | Sammy is five and the only child of a mother with schizophrenia. She is devoted to Sammy and cares for him well as long as she takes her medication. Sammy has just started school and the school says that, despite appearing chatty and polite, they feel he is an anxious child. He finds it hard to play with other children and is clingy with the teachers. He says he sleeps in his mum's bed because of the ghosts in the house. She has started turning up during the school day to check he is okay. Sammy's needs are ... | **Health**
Maintaining health
To maintain existing good health
A healthy diet
Opportunities for exercise
Access to health services
Routine health surveillance
To better understand mum's illness
Individual work to identify need
Mum needs a mental health assessment!
Assessment of Sammy's mental health/attachment in order to provide appropriate services and the impact of his mum's mental health

Education
Stability and security in education placement to reduce anxiety
To learn and be exposed to age-appropriate learning opportunities and experiences
Needs to feel secure in school
Social opportunities
To attend school
Support from classroom assistant
Establish what school actually means to Sammy
Educational Psychologist assessment

Emotional and behavioural development
Self-esteem
Relationship-building
Play and self-occupancy skills
Stability
Security
Boundaries. Appropriate separation from his mum
Age-appropriate socialising – free from responsibility to and for mother
Friendships
Needs security and to feel safe
Assessment of attachment issues
Referral to young carers' project

Identity
To have a clear sense of his own identity
Needs to establish one, e.g. life story work
A sense of growing independence from mother
Freedom to pursue personal identity separate from his mother
Mother to be secure and mentally well in order to focus on him
Assess if any issues

Family and social relationships
Exposure to relatives and friends
Opportunities for wider experience in safe environment
Support to come to terms with mother's illness
Needs security and probably wider network, e.g. community/family
Assessment of what family networks there are?

Social presentation
Psychological assessment
Referral to after-school club

Self-care skills
Needs to fit into peer group
To be relaxed, secure in self |

Practice development 4 session: Needs analysis

Aim

To introduce a model for needs-led analysis and planning for children and their families; and to provide an opportunity to test this out in practice.

Method

Introduction

■ Introduce the theme of the session by showing Presentation 4, sildes 37–40. Download from www.ncb.org.uk/resources/support). Preferably expand on it in the following ways.

- Mention that inspection reports have commented that it is not always clear how services provided meet needs.

- Make the point that consideration of needs is very relevant to the assessment of family and friends (explain, if necessary, that it is important when assessing a child's needs to look at whether the family can meet them and what kind of support they would require to do so).

- Explain that, if the child's needs are stated explicitly, it helps children and their parents to understand what must be done to meet needs, and what the purpose of the intervention is.

- In analysing the situation it is helpful to remain focused on the child's needs rather than being drawn too much into the parents' difficulties.

Stage 1 of the decision-making

■ Invite the participants to form groups of three to five.

■ Distribute the Case studies Danny and Sammy so that each group has either Danny or Sammy. Also give out some sticky notes to each group.

■ Ask the participants to look at the case study they have been given and, in their pairs or groups, to identify all the child's needs under each of the developmental dimensions of the assessment triangle. Make it clear that they should record **each need** on a separate sticky note.

■ Tell them they have 10 minutes to complete this.

■ Meanwhile, prepare two flip charts, one for Danny, one for Sammy. (Or, if you have prepared your own case studies, record their names instead.) Write the seven dimension titles on each flip chart, leaving space under each dimension title for participants to attach sticky notes.

■ After 10 minutes, ask participants to come to the flip chart and place sticky notes under the child's name and specific dimensions.

■ Offer feedback on the activity. Comment positively on where clear needs have been identified (such as the need to increase self-esteem, feeling safe, access to peer relationships) and also note where services have been identified (such as paediatric assessment, counselling, family centre). Invite participants to disagree if they wish, and reassure them that picking up on issues is not meant as personal criticism.

■ Give information on the theory that underpins this activity, referring to the notes above if necessary.

Stage 2 of the decision-making

■ Give the participants an example of what an outcome (in relation to a need) might be, for example:

– **Need** – child to have social relationships with peers.

– **Outcome** – Child has two friends at school with whom she/he regularly plays with at break times OR child attends playgroup twice a week and successfully mixes socially with children his/her age.

■ Remind participants that they are not to identify services to meet needs – yet.

■ Invite participants to form pairs. Check that each couple is focusing on the case of one child and are not concerning themselves with siblings. Ask them to identify up to three needs first, then work from left to right on the needs and outcomes form (page 39) completing the boxes: why the need is currently a priority; what they think will happen if the need is not met; what a good outcome will look like; what SMART objectives along the way will help to achieve the outcome; and what interventions, actions or services could meet this need (including actions by family members or the child themselves). Alternatively if time is short, one need identified in one of the case study examples could be worked through.

■ Encourage participants to record an action or service even if no such service currently exists. If this is the case ask them to describe such a service. The purpose of the last part of the exercise is to encourage participants to be more actively engaged in making suggestions within their agencies about the type of services required to meet the identified needs of children in the area. This might seem unfair in the current climate of service cuts but there is more likelihood of services evolving if those at the front line of practice are able to better articulate what the gaps are. It also might encourage participants to think more creatively about how needs could be met.

■ Conclude this part by mentioning resilience as a key aspect of the desired outcomes. Explain that the planned outcome should not just be to minimise the damage to children but to positively promote their well-being. So practitioners would need to think about and include preparation for any separations; and ways of promoting trusting relationships, friendships and success at school, hobbies and interests.

Feedback

■ Ask participants how they felt the activity went.

■ Ask: Was it hard to focus on the child's needs?

■ Invite each group to give one example of a child's need, a planned outcome and a service to meet it.

■ Ask: Do you feel that slowing down the decision-making stages added anything to their usual mode of operation?

- Ask: Did it mean that they might select different types of services or different constellations of service to meet children's needs?

- Invite participants to consider how the clear focus on needs might assist with analysis throughout the assessment – for example, in terms of agreeing the approach with the family or explaining a particular course of action in a report.

- Ask: How might this approach be helpful to you in day-to-day practice? And in supervision, arguing for resources, etc.

Risk and resilience

All of us can probably identify at least one child with whom we have worked, who, despite facing multiple difficulties, abuse, neglect or losses seems to have been able to maintain some equilibrium and has emerged, perhaps not completely unscathed, but with their survival mechanism intact and maintaining hope for the future. What exactly is it that protects these children better than others in similar circumstances? Resilience is a theory developed to describe the interaction of internal and external factors that can provide a buffer against the more harmful effects of severe or cumulative negative experiences. This section identifies factors that increase resilience and explores the application of a framework to assist in assessment and intervention, to reduce risk and promote resilience in children and young people.

Research into the concept of resilience has been ongoing since the early 1970s when Emmy Werner began a longtitudonal study of children growing up in poverty in Hawaii. And, in 1973 Garmezy explored the experiences of children living with parental schizophrenia. In both studies a significant minority of children fared better than others and seemed to exhibit characteristics that provided them with some protection. The theory has further evolved, with significant contributions from British contributors such as Rutter (1993), Gilligan (2001, 2009) and Daniel and Wassell (2002).

For a long time, services have tended to focus on vulnerable children in terms of the 'risks of significant harm' that they face or the 'needs' they have that are not being met at the time. This is still the case, although the emphasis, whether it be 'risk driven' or 'need driven', shifts over time. Currently there is a greater tendency to consider the strengths and protective factors within families (supported by the *Framework for Assessment of Children in Need and their Families*, Department of Health 2000; and more recently by the *Common Assessment Framework*, HM Government 2006b).

Resilience theory, informed by ecological theory (Bronfenbrenner 1989) operates at the multiple levels of the child, family and external environment. The factors associated with resilience are defined as intrinsic (associated with individual qualities such as temperament or intelligence) and extrinsic (located at the outer ecological levels of family and wider community) (Daniel and Wassell 2002). Critically, it is the dynamic interaction of these factors that creates resilience.

> *Resilience is a dynamic process involving shifting balances of protective and vulnerability forces in different risk contexts and at different developmental stages.*
> *(Luthar and Zelazo in Luthar 2003)*

Gilligan (2009) refers to resilience 'residing more in the quality of the contexts surrounding the person, than in the person'. This underlines the importance of the influence of others in promoting or undermining resilience in children.

There are different manifestations of 'resilience', for example there are those who succeed despite high risk status; those who exhibit maturity and coping in the face of chronic stress; and those who have suffered extreme trauma but have recovered and prospered (Newman and Blackburn 2002). Resilience is not fixed but changes over time, often showing itself in later life following an earlier phase where difficulties in coping were exhibited. Whilst longitudinal studies show that many children recover from short-lived problems, when adversities are continuous and severe and there are no observable protective factors, resilience is much rarer.

> *there is ... no simple association between stress and gain. Some stressors may trigger resilient assets in children, others may compound chronic difficulties. If children are subjected to a relentless stream of multiple adversities, negative consequences are highly likely to follow.*
> *(Newman and Blackburn 2002, p.4)*

46

Poor early experiences don't necessarily dictate future outcomes, however, as compensatory interventions can trigger responses that enhance resilience.

Resilience theory has been criticised by some for potentially overlooking less visible factors that could be being stored up to create problems for children as they move into adulthood. For instance, the apparently 'high achieving' child' may be viewed as having survived their early experiences relatively unscathed, when in fact their emotional life, confidence or self-esteem may be affected in ways that are neither seen, reported or considered. Similarly, unconscious psychological processes such as dissociation, developed as a protective mechanism in situations of violence or abuse may be misinterpreted as signs of resilience. Also an overemphasis on 'coping' could lead to suppression of healthy and necessary responses to trauma and loss such as expression of grief, anxiety and sadness. The danger of misinterpretation could mean that children who continue to need intensive and sensitive intervention in order to support their recovery may miss out and subsequently become more vulnerable as a result. A useful perspective to help with such dilemmas can be to remind ourselves that the purpose of services and interventions should be to elicit the internal strengths, resilience, motivations and goals that already exist within individuals and families.

Given some of the other concerns about the notion of resilience, it is important to be clear in our thinking and in what we communicate when we discuss resilience with other professionals, with families and in reports. It is not so much about someone's capacity to manage, as about the associations between the presence of some factors (often referred to as 'protective factors') with long-term good outcomes.

The purpose of risk assessments in social work is closely associated with the prevention of existing or future significant harm and this involves the weighing up of both positive and negative factors in children's circumstances. In relation to analysis in assessment an understanding of 'resilience' is helpful in terms of providing an evidence-based framework within which to consider judgements about the interplay of risk and protective factors within children's lives, their families and their wider circumstances. Of course no framework exists that can reduce this to a simple task. As Turney and others (2008) noted in their study of social work assessments of children in need:

> Resilience is a difficult notion to conceptualise and to apply.

Turney and others (2008) noted the dangers of over-emphasising resilience and highlighted the need for better professional education in key areas of resilience, self-esteem, identity and attachment.

Despite this there are a commonly agreed range of factors which are shown to promote resilience in children and using this understanding in the assessment process alongside a consideration of factors creating adversity and risk for children should lead to more inclusive and imaginative recommendations that explore how positives can be strengthened and deficits reduced. Such a focus can help in moving from assessment to intervention and can help to reduce the sorts of 'additional harm' that can compound difficult experiences, perhaps needlessly, when some attention given to an aspect of someone's life or needs could relieve their situation or distress.

Factors that enhance children's resilience

The International Resilience Project has sought to build a universal understanding of resilience since the early 1990s. The three sources of resilience defined by the project, I have, I am and I can are briefly described below (Grotberg 1995):

I have: people who trust and love me, set limits, model behaviour, promote autonomy and are available to protect and educate.

I am: likeable, respectful towards and concerned for others, taking responsibility for myself and optimistic for the future.

I can: communicate about problems, solve problems, exercise self-control in my behaviour and know when to act, when to seek help and who from.

For practitioners seeking to undertake assessments of children's needs these concepts can helpfully be applied alongside the three domains of *The Framework for the Assessment of Children in Need and their Families* (Department of Health and others 2000). The following points, adapted from Sawyer (2009), expand on these concepts.

The child has a secure relationship with one reliable adult

For all children and young people facing difficulties of any kind having a relationship with a key supportive family member is the most powerful positive factor influencing their ability to cope. This is due both to the attachment relationship, which provides the child with the foundation for their self-esteem and for developing relationships with others, and to the increased likelihood of them receiving the care and support they need practically and emotionally.

Influence of another stable adult figure or figures

Beyond the child's family or home environment, the presence of a committed mentor or positive and interested adult outside the family is also an important positive factor. Such a relationship can provide the child or young person with encouragement – much needed attention, consistency, a sense of stability and more. This may come from either informal networks such as members of the wider family, neighbours or friends' parents or from more formal sources such as teachers or other professionals.

Positive social support networks and a social role

Support networks such as friendships, clubs, and membership of groups or attendance at faith-based institutions can all help children develop a sense of being valued or 'valuable'. Participation in extracurricular activities, which children enjoy or are good at, can promote their self-esteem.

Positive school experiences

Linked with the two points above, schools provide the opportunities for forming friendships with peers, with other adults and for developing social skills, interests, talents and self-esteem. Educational success is an additional factor, which if experienced is associated with children who fare better later in life due to the opportunities it gives them, as well as to the increased self-esteem, knowledge and ways of understanding the world that help them to interact more positively within it.

A sense that one's own efforts can make a difference

If children can be enabled to exert any influence on their own circumstances, however small, this can enhance their well-being. Being helped to make choices, and being consulted and asked about their views, can all promote their sense that they can make a difference. Also, a sense that problems can be overcome is very important to young people becoming proactive and optimistic in their approach to life.

Personal or 'inherent' qualities

Children with good verbal skills, good cognitive ability, the absence of neurobiological problems, and who demonstrate autonomy, sociability and good self-esteem, tend to fare better than children who do not have these qualities. The extent to which some of these 'qualities' can be influenced varies of course. A child's behaviour, confidence and ability are not static, however. With support and opportunities, some children who are regarded as 'unsociable' or 'inarticulate' for example, may demonstrate significant changes over time.

A child's own 'coping' skills

The more children are able to understand and express their feelings, the more they can make sense of their situations and survive them with less harm done. In families where feelings are denied, where emotions are seen as volatile or silenced, it is much harder for children to develop such positive responses. Interventions that bolster a child's ability to recognise and name feelings, as well as to express them and ask for help, will enhance their resilience. Some social situations and opportunities, such as activities that are challenging but achievable, can also provide children with opportunities to develop coping skills.

A child's view of themselves

Children who see themselves as separate from the problems in their family tend to fare better than those who believe that they are a part of the problems and that their problems are a part of them. Children who, while knowing they are part of a family, see themselves as distinct individuals with separate feelings, qualities and potential, are likely to have better outcomes.

Plans for the future

Children who can imagine their futures and who are encouraged and supported to make positive plans about their future are more likely to do well. Plans in the short term are also important as they provide things to look forward to, both with and without the rest of their family.

Early and compensatory experiences

The older the child is at the onset of the difficulties in their family or circumstances, the greater the range of coping resources they will have developed. Therefore, less early exposure to problems increases their life chances. For example, where there are substantial periods in which parents care for their children well and the children feel loved, they will fare better than if neglect or harm is chronic and long term.

Familial and parenting characteristics that enhance resilience

A confiding relationship with a partner or with others

When parents under stress have a partner who they can share their thoughts, feelings and experiences with and with whom they can be honest, their well-being and in turn their parenting capacity is enhanced. Parents who have positive relationships with others are more likely to be able to develop a positive connection with their child. Being able to listen to their partners or others and reciprocate within relationships enhances this further.

Cohesive and consistent parental relationship

The absence of parental conflict is associated with better outcomes for children. If parents are able to present a 'united front' to their children, showing that they agree and are consistent in the boundaries they set and the plans they have, this helps children by providing the consistency they need and reducing confusion, insecurity and uncertainty. Consistently enforced rules are another resilience factor within parenting; and a cohesive relationship (where there is more than one parent) will support this.

Parental self-esteem

Parents who (with or without support) are able to value themselves and see what their positive qualities and abilities are and what they mean to other people are better able to parent effectively. Therefore interventions and informal support that seeks to enhance, rather than undermine, self-esteem are very important.

Role models

Parents, other adults and siblings demonstrate acceptable behaviour inside the family and in their interaction with others. This includes styles of communication, styles of dress, moral attitudes and belief systems.

Adequate finances and employment opportunities

Families who have sufficient finances available to them fare better than those who don't. Increased resources mean more access to support for individuals within the family or for the whole family. These resources include more suitable housing; social and leisure opportunities; breaks and respite; private counselling; and access to support with childcare or even with domestic tasks.

Constructive coping styles and deliberate parental actions to minimise adversity for children

The coping strategies employed by parents impact directly or indirectly on the way the child manages their experiences and emotions. If parents are productive, focusing on positives, dealing with problems, and children likely to do the same.

Openness and good communication

Whatever the nature of the problems within families, if there is an atmosphere of openness in which thoughts, feelings and uncertainties can be safely expressed, the outcomes for children, and the wider family, will be supported by this.

Knowledge of 'protective factors'

If parents know about the things that make a difference to children and to the outcomes for them, they are more able to utilise them (Velleman 2004). Helping parents to recognise the importance of certain factors, such as children's engagement in hobbies or the importance of observing family occasions and keeping some routines, is helpful and potentially empowering.

Community factors that enhance resilience

Cultural connectedness, values and identity

Children and young people who see themselves as part of their community, who are linked in with groups and services, fare better than those who are disconnected. For example, if a positive identity or valued local culture exists within a community, or a child identifies positively as a member of an ethnic or religious group, this relates to better outcomes and a more positive identity. A socially rich environment in which people are inclined to look out for each other, intervene and help out is associated with better outcomes for children and families.

Access to health, education, welfare and other services

The child, independently or through the family, will benefit from consistent services to meet the needs the family cannot fulfil – hospitals and doctors, schools and teachers, social services, and police and fire protection, or the equivalent of these services.

Promoting positive change

Knowledge of resilience or 'protective' factors is not in itself enough to influence the experiences of children. However, if such knowledge is translated into support and actions aimed directly at influencing such factors, this can promote positive change. At the individual level, this could mean placing more emphasis on facilitating a child's access to a supportive adult, social or leisure opportunity or helping a parent understand and act on the knowledge of what is important for their child. When it comes to planning and shaping services, such knowledge adds weight to the importance of supporting extended family members, working more proactively with fathers and linking responses more effectively with schools or community resources. On the whole, the literature shows informal support to be more helpful to families than formal professional involvement, it is also worth services considering how they can better:

foster the characteristics of responsiveness, flexibility, reliability and supportiveness that characterise family and community supports

Olsen and Wates 2003, p.26

Practice tool 5: Resilience/vulnerability matrix

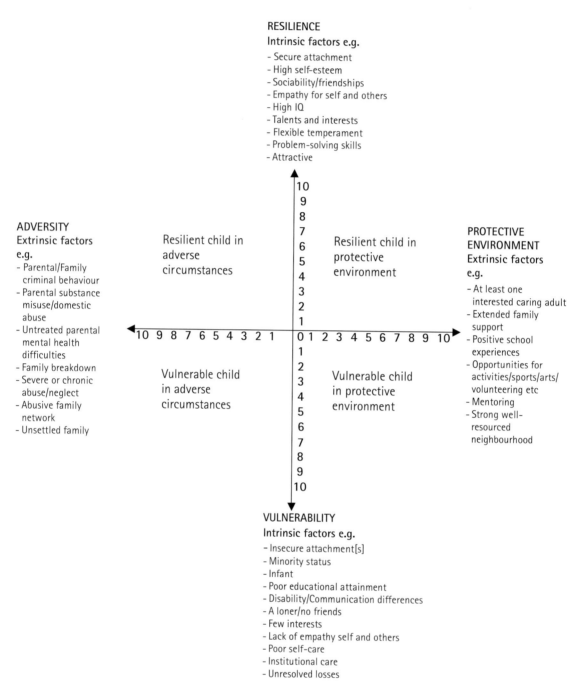

RESILIENCE
Intrinsic factors e.g.

- Secure attachment
- High self-esteem
- Sociability/friendships
- Empathy for self and others
- High IQ
- Talents and interests
- Flexible temperament
- Problem-solving skills
- Attractive

ADVERSITY
Extrinsic factors
e.g.
- Parental/Family criminal behaviour
- Parental substance misuse/domestic abuse
- Untreated parental mental health difficulties
- Family breakdown
- Severe or chronic abuse/neglect
- Abusive family network
- Unsettled family

Resilient child in adverse circumstances

Resilient child in protective environment

PROTECTIVE ENVIRONMENT
Extrinsic factors
e.g.

- At least one interested caring adult
- Extended family support
- Positive school experiences
- Opportunities for activities/sports/arts/ volunteering etc
- Mentoring
- Strong well-resourced neighbourhood

10 9 8 7 6 5 4 3 2 1

0 1 2 3 4 5 6 7 8 9 10

10 9 8 7 6 5 4 3 2 1
1 2 3 4 5 6 7 8 9 10

Vulnerable child in adverse circumstances

Vulnerable child in protective environment

VULNERABILITY
Intrinsic factors e.g.

- Insecure attachment[s]
- Minority status
- Infant
- Poor educational attainment
- Disability/Communication differences
- A loner/no friends
- Few interests
- Lack of empathy self and others
- Poor self-care
- Institutional care
- Unresolved losses

Based on figure in Horwarth, J and others (2000) The Child's World: Assessing children in need – World Training & Development Pack. London: NSPCC

Using the resilience matrix in assessment and planning with children, young people and families

The aim of the matrix is to develop an understanding of how the different factors and circumstances in a child's life are interacting to contribute to their current vulnerability or resilience and to use this understanding to develop plans to increase the resilience-promoting factors and reduce those that contribute to vulnerability. The matrix can be used visually to explain and to engage children, their carers and other professionals in building an understanding of a way forward for the child.

Completion of the matrix requires the practitioner to have a working knowledge of resilience theory and the factors that contribute to the different axes of the matrix. A good starting point would be to read Daniel, Wassell and Gilligan (2010) *Child Development for Child Care and Protection Workers* (chapters 4 and 5).

Sufficient information will need to have been accumulated from assessment or other interaction with a child, their carers, family and involved professionals. Each axis of the matrix contains a scale from 0 to 10, with 0 being an absence of factors contributing to that domain of the matrix and 10 being the highest incidence of contributory factors.

Taking each axis in turn, the information that has been gathered is scored on the 0–10 scale. For example, for a child with a secure attachment, good problem-solving skills, popular with peers, high IQ and doing well at school this would most likely lead to a high score on the **resilience** axis of the matrix. If, however, that child has been self-harming for some time and this is becoming more severe over time, and they are developing anxiety problems that are interfering with their day to day life, a score to reflect this would be placed on the **vulnerability** axis. If the same young person is living in a family situation with domestic abuse, parental mental ill health and financial insecurity this would indicate a significant score on the **adversity** axis, but if they also have good relationships with teachers and other adults and made good use of support and advice offered from the school counsellor this would be noted on the **protective environment** axis. The matrix is most useful when used as an interactive tool with children and young people as active agents in the process.

There are no right and wrong answers and the scoring will be a matter of professional judgement, indeed whenever we use this tool in training there are vigorous debates as to the impact, harmful or beneficial of various factors in children's lives. The completion of the matrix only represents the understanding of the child's situation at that time and by those involved in constructing it. It will be informed by theory, research, practice wisdom, local knowledge and information gleaned from a range of sources, including the child themselves. The process of considering and plotting the information is in itself a useful process and requires thoughtfulness and possibly debate if being done with others, but there is another stage that can create a powerful visual map. Once all of the axes have been considered and plotted, the points can be joined with a drawn line to create a shape that will be spread across the four domains (located more within some than others). See illustration of Peter and Liam on page 57. This visual map can help in assessment and planning by providing a snapshot, but can also be useful for recording progress if completed at various intervals.

Where the shape sits predominantly in the top right-hand quadrant of the two axes this suggest that the child is both resilient and protected and more likely to be able to recover from any difficulties they face. This is the safest area for children to be and universal services can support and build on these positive factors.

Where the shape sits predominantly in the lower right quadrant this indicates that the child is protected, but for whatever reason also vulnerable. This will mean that the planning for this child should focus on maintaining the support whilst building up their resilience. An example of this could be a child with a communication difference as a result of disability placed with long-term foster carers. The carers may need help in developing their communication skills whilst the young person is supported in their use of technology to enhance their communications. Children in this quadrant will need specific support if their protection is removed, but a combination of universal, targeted and specialist services will work to increase their resilience.

Where the shape sits predominantly in the top left quadrant, this indicates a child who exhibits signs of resilience whilst remaining in adverse circumstances. These are the children that targeted and specialist services should be working with to increase the level of protection, in partnership with the child and their family, whether by raising them from poverty or taking action to safeguard against abuse. One criticism of this model is that resilient children in risky situations may be ignored as relatively safe. It is crucial to recognise that no matter how resilient children may be, there will be times when the risks are too severe to ignore and the presence of resilience factors should never be an excuse for lack of attention or inaction.

If the shape sits predominantly in the lower left corner of the graph it indicates the most vulnerable child who does not have resilience or factors within their environment to provide protection. This child will need intensive specialist intervention. As well as identifying the associated risk this model allows us to develop care plans in two directions – to increase the level of protection and to improve children's resilience, improving the chances of reducing risk.

The resilience/vulnerability matrix

The resilience/vulnerability matrix on page 52 provides a framework for weighing up and considering factors that create adversity for children and increase their vulnerability alongside those factors that research has demonstrated can contribute to increased resilience in children and young people. The impact of adversities is known to be cumulative over time and therefore the response to them also needs to be multi-layered and cumulative. The matrix does not provide easy answers or a simplistic way of understanding the fine balance of contributory factors to outcomes for children but it can help in creating a visual representation of how the factors are interacting and what actions or interventions may provide protection and stimulate the growth of resilience.

Case study: Johnson family

Name	Relationship	Age	Information
Emma Johnson	Mother	29	Single parent. White British
Katie Brown	Daughter	15	Currently living at maternal aunt's after falling out with her mother. Regular contact with father
Peter Brown	Son	13	Contact with father monthly. White British
Liam Johnson	Son	5	Speech delay and chronic eczema and asthma, which requires support Sporadic contact with putative father, Jojo Mixed heritage African/White British
Steve Brown	Father of Katie and Peter	33	Regular contact with both children. Consistent and supportive figure in the life of the family. White British
Jojo Kwame	Putative father of Liam	36	Irregular visitor, contact characterised by stress. Very unsupportive. Black African (Ghanaian)

Emma has lived in a town in Essex all her life. She spent some periods of time in care as a child although always returned home and is still in close contact with her mother and brothers and sisters. Her father died nine years ago.

Children's services have had involvement with Emma and her children since a child protection investigation when Katie was three as a result of Emma's increasingly erratic behaviour, poor home conditions and Katie being left home alone on more than one occasion. This led to Katie being on the child protection register for a year. After referral to her GP and a psychiatrist, Emma was diagnosed as suffering from bipolar disorder. She eventually engaged with adult mental health services and began taking medication for the condition after which her health improved and a network of support was established. Support and intervention has been provided by a local family centre at various times and Mary, the manager there, has dropped in to see the family from time to time informally over the years.

Emma has maintained good health and has remained on medication for significant periods since her first hospitalisation, during which time her care of the children has been good. Since then, there have been two occasions when Emma has become ill and has needed in-patient psychiatric care: once, briefly, after her father died and, for a longer period, six months after the birth of Liam. On both occasions there was a period of weeks or months prior to the hospital admission when her mental health was deteriorating and various agencies expressed concern. On both occasions during the manic or high phase of her illness, Emma and her children were put at risk by her erratic behaviour. On the second occasion Liam was placed in foster care for six months, but returned home when Emma's condition stabilised.

Ellie and Peter's father lived with Emma until Peter was two, and has remained in regular contact with Ellie and Peter. He has married and had other children and has been a stable figure in Ellie and Peter's life and has been supportive to Emma.

Liam's father Jojo has been in contact occasionally. His relationship with Emma was very short and they never lived together. He has tried previously to gain custody of Liam, but failed due, in part, to several convictions for violence and domestic abuse. He is very unsympathetic to Emma's illness and refers to her as 'mad'. His contact with the family is characterised by arguments and threats. Formal contact arrangements have been set up in past, but have broken down due to Jojo's erratic attendance.

Emma lives close to her mother, who helps out sometimes but who has quite a few health problems of her own. She loves her grandchildren, but can be quite critical of Emma, not really understanding her mental health difficulties and stating that she is just 'being wilful' when she is ill.

Katie recently moved into her Aunt Helen's house after she broke down at school and said she was exhausted trying to help her mum look after the two younger children and worrying about her mum's health. Her aunt Helen offered to provide her with a home while she was studying for her GCSEs, with Emma's agreement, but since Katie moved out things have take a turn for the worse at home.

Concerns have been raised by health agencies about Liam's missed health and speech therapy appointments and his school as a result of his eczema and asthma being out of control and his forgetting his asthma inhaler. He is often very late for school and turns up dressed in mismatched clothes. His teacher has expressed concern about him being isolated in class and generally disconnected from other children but with fairly frequent noisy, angry outbursts that make the other children wary of him. The school has begun to wonder if his behaviour might place him on the autistic spectrum and have tried to engage Emma in discussion about this, to no avail. Liam loves singing, however, and has a very clear singing voice. He seems to be very attached to his granny, who picks him up from school sometimes. Emma has often said to Liam's teacher that he is much harder to care for than either of the other two were when young and that she thinks he is a really naughty boy and 'just like his dad'.

Peter's school is concerned about the fact that he has missed quite a few days recently and has asked the EWO to try and visit to find out why. He has been a very good attender in the past and has been a popular boy who is well liked by teachers. He has shown promise in drama and creative writing and his recent absences are uncharacteristic. He has talked previously to his form tutor about his mother's illness and has recently expressed concern about her and his younger brother to the tutor and the EWO. Peter has several good friends at school and he attends a local drama club where he has been involved in musical theatre shows. Peter spends one weekend a month with his father and his new family 30 miles away.

Today, Peter went to the family centre where the family had received help in the past to see the manager and ask her to contact the community psychiatric nurse to get them to visit his mum who he said is 'getting poorly again'. He told the centre manager that his dad has offered for him to come and live with him but that he feels his mum needs him at the moment. He also said that the house is a terrible mess, his mum is going out all the time and that the bailiffs came round recently due to debts his mother had built up but his mum made them all hide from them.

For the purposes of illustration the information relating to Peter and Liam is plotted on the matrix on the following page. This interpretation is open to debate and discussion. In a real-life situation there would be considerably more variables and pieces of information available for consideration.

Peter (the dotted line) is shown to be fairly resilient due to his age, a fairly secure attachment to his mother, having experienced a number of years of a reasonably secure base, likely to have a strong sense of identity, a good relationship with his father, having a problem-solving approach, good help-seeking behaviour, a sense of responsibility, ability to make friends, intelligence, talents and interests. He has some protective factors in the adults who are looking out for him, the fact that he has good relationships at school and has talents and interests outside school. There is some vulnerability in that he has experienced loss and change in his earlier life, he still needs emotional and practical support to reach maturity and he is still too young to be independent. There is considerable adversity as a result of his mother's longstanding mental illness and the recent change as a result of Katie leaving home, the additional responsibility he faces and the material and financial circumstances at home.

Resilience/vulnerability matrix for Peter and Liam

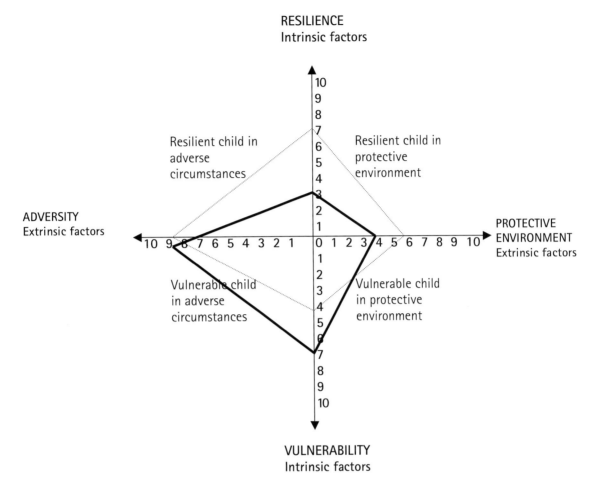

Liam (represented by the heavier line) is much less resilient and, therefore, more vulnerable due to his age, his health and communication needs, the lack of a stable relationship with his father, his mixed heritage origins and experience of racism or his identity needs not being met, his experience of separation from his mother and of foster care as an infant, his mother's ambivalence towards him, his communication needs and his isolation from peers. His love of singing and talent in this area may provide some resilience in future but at present the vulnerability factors are more apparent. There are some protective factors in that his older brother expresses concern about him, he has a close relationship with his grandmother, and his mother can care well enough for him when she is well, but there is considerable adversity in his life as a result of his mother's illness, the relationship breakdowns in the past, his father's behaviour and the family's material and financial circumstances.

Using the matrix to identify the resilience, vulnerability adversity and protective factors will help in working inclusively with the family to construct a plan provide a protective environment for both children with the appropriate degree of specialist support and encouragement according to each of their individual needs.

Practice development session 5: Risk and resilience

Aim

To explore the application of resilience theory and the resilience/vulnerability matrix to assessment and planning with children young people and their families.

Method

■ Introduce the concept of resilience by asking participants to think about someone they know, whether in their professional or personal lives, who despite having experienced adversity and hardship in childhood has gone on to recover and thrive. Ask them to identify what they believe the factors were that contributed to this person's recovery.

■ Then ask them to pair up with one other person and share the story. Ask them to work together to try and separate out the factors that were within the child/person and those that were external factors, in the family or wider community. Ask for general feedback.

■ Give some input on resilience using Presentation 5, slides 42–48, or give a handout on resilience from another source, and discuss as a group. Ask about participants' existing knowledge and understanding of the theory, make links to the assessment framework and how it fits well with the framework as an ecological theory that integrates personal, family and community influences on outcomes for children.

■ Give out the resilience/vulnerability matrix from page 52 and discuss how the matrix helps in building an understanding of how the different factors interact. Stress how this can assist in both assessment and planning interventions due to the recognition of the cumulative influence of negative and positive influences. Make the point that placing scores on the different axes of the matrix is a matter of professional judgement and will be influenced by a range of factors and that it will be a very individual picture for each child. Stress the importance of recognising that even children within the same family can be more or less resilient for a number of different reasons. Ask someone to volunteer to talk through with the group where they might have plotted the person they were discussing in the first exercise. Have a ready prepared example to use if there are no volunteers.

■ Break the group into smaller groups of three or four participants. Either use the Peter and Liam case study on page 55 or one of your choice or a piece of video (for example, case scenario 3: Sean and Helen from *The Developing World of the Child* training pack video NSPCC 2007) and ask people in their groups to identify the resilience, vulnerability, protective and adversity factors for each of the children. If using the case study in this book, do not show the participants the worked example of the matrix with Peter and Liam until after the exercise. Suggest that they spend time discussing and debating their view of how much each piece of information would contribute to the children's resilience or vulnerability. Ask them to complete the matrix by joining up the numbers to form a shape. Once this is done take feedback about where each child predominantly sits on the matrix and why. There are likely to be different views, some quite strongly held, so allow for some debate and where possible relate back to the theory and the evidence base. Show the worked example with the accompanying notes. This is likely to stimulate further debate.

■ As an optional additional stage you could ask participants to take the role of different characters within the case study family (if using the video or another case study you will need to decide who these characters are) and do a 'talking heads' exercise where you ask each 'character' to think for five minutes about what the concerns and preoccupations of their character would be. Then set up a circle of chairs for each character to sit in and move around the circle asking each character to speak in turn about their concerns, feelings, worries, hopes etc. in the first person. This is not an interactive role play and the characters do not communicate with each other. Once everyone has spoken ask other participants to comment on the issues it raised for them. If the group are keen and the 'characters' willing, you could extend this section by allowing participants to ask questions of the characters about what they want to happen, what worries them most, etc. Although this is fictionalised it can be a very powerful exercise. Then have some discussion about how you can ensure that children's views and feelings can be kept at the heart of assessment and planning, how they can be helped to be active agents in the process.

■ Ask people to identify actions/interventions aimed at increasing the protective and resilience factors for the children whilst reducing the adversity and vulnerability factors. Remind them to think about how they would involve the children and their carers in setting and reviewing objectives and discuss some of the resources/tools and materials they might use to help achieve the objectives (remembering that some of these resources will be within the child's existing family or circle. It is important to acknowledge here that just because the interventions have been identified it doesn't mean that will automatically work and the matrix will need to be used to help in monitoring and reviewing progress and if necessary adjusting plans.

Signs of safety

This section looks at the need to do more to ensure that assessments are not too skewed by an over-concentration on risk of harm; and that families' strengths are sufficiently acknowledged and harnessed throughout the course of assessment and intervention. It goes on to include a brief introduction to the Signs of safety approach put forward by Turnell and Edwards (1999).

The last few sections have looked at the ease with which social workers can unwittingly jump to decisions that are unduly influenced by the context in which they are operating, such as service constraints and fear of making mistakes. This tendency extends to the whole approach that social workers take to their assessments and to their relationships with all family members being assessed.

Whilst a desire to work in partnership with families and service users is hardly a new idea, it is still, in reality, hard to translate meaningfully into practice.

In recent years it has been widely acknowledged and demonstrated, for example in *Child Protection: Messages from research* (DH 1995), that in England the emphasis in child care social work has been more on child protection than on preventative family support approaches. Whilst the *Framework for Assessment of Children in Need and their Families* (Department of Health and others 2000) is intended to enshrine a needs-based approach, where strengths are considered in tandem with risk of harm, pressure on services means that often the bulk of allocated cases are those where some risk of harm or severe needs are present. With this, the tendency has perhaps been to over-emphasise investigative and forensic procedures.

Parton (1996, in Turnell and Edwards 1999) argues that this:

> *effectively becomes a blaming system, the primary purpose being to establish who is accountable for any given incident.*

It is hardly surprising that true partnership-working with parents and family members is such a difficult area when the stakes in children and families' social work are so high. One of the greatest conundrums of child protection, the authors of the Signs of safety approach argue, is:

> *How to recognise the occasional families that cannot be assisted or coerced to provide increased safety, without demonising excessive numbers of other families with the same, though inappropriate label.*

When social workers are concerned about a child's welfare, an inadequate understanding of the parent whom they consider to be responsible for that child, can often lead to skewed and over-simplistic conclusions. If a child's experience is in the range of the 'thresholds' of likely or actual significant harm, social workers don't want to mess about. They need to do something about it. To get answers and clarity, so as to act as is their duty. Legal and policy constraints form almost invisible walls around their focus and thinking. This is for a good reason. If they did not have the clarity of message – that is, *if a child is or is likely to be suffering significant harm it is our legal duty to protect them* – then their good intentions of fairness, and natural resistance to coping with uncertainty, could lead to them becoming paralysed by that uncertainty or 'woolly' in thinking, and therefore to becoming variable in their priorities and responses. While the social workers sit and wonder, more children might get harmed; or those being harmed may not get help from social workers to prevent, minimise or stop them from coming to harm.

Partnership therefore, whilst its worthiness is indisputable, can easily be in danger of being only surface deep. The social worker might, for example, show a parent the report they write and give the parent sufficient time to comment, suggest alternatives and have their views recorded before signing it. The social worker might give the parent information about their rights, try to involve them in formulating and carrying out protection plans or facilitate a Family Group Conference, none of which are to be minimised. However, just as often social workers might gradually 'accept' that they 'cannot' involve a semi-absent, alleged substance-misusing father. They give up on him and, after deciding that the mother (who tells a health visitor one thing and the social worker another) is not being honest or 'able to work in partnership', they start making statements (literally or figuratively) about her denying her problem, lacking insight, and being 'unable to put her child's needs first'. Such statements are weighty and have powerful implications, but are in danger of being used perhaps too readily or with insufficient qualification.

Turnell and Edwards (1999) highlighted feedback, gained from parents in consumer studies, in which parents described the feeling of being seen as a 'case', especially in evidence gathering interviews. The emphasis on identifying deficits and weaknesses – rather than strengths and resources – contributes to families' defensiveness; and a steady stream of professionals focusing on what is wrong can undermine a family's sense of its capacities and capabilities (Ban 1992, in Turnell and Edwards 1999). They felt that if they were identified as bad parents early on, it was very difficult if not impossible to get workers to see them differently or as 'capable' later on.

These issues are not easily solved and good intentions alone are not enough on their own to mitigate against the many and real pressures on social workers, which may lead to giving up on partnership too easily. The following approach is just one example of a model social workers can draw from to help in the conscious pursuit of balance and partnership within their work.

The Signs of safety approach

Signs of Safety: A solution and safety orientated approach to child protection (Turnell and Edwards 1999) has 'promoting partnership' as its underpinning principle. The approach emphasises the need to try and establish 'collaboration', with service users as opposed to a 'helping relationship'. The approach involves: *turning away from deficits and focusing on the discovery of resources, however small, to expose building blocks for change.*

The approach was born out of the Teen Link project in Perth, Australia in the early 1990s. There were only three workers who had a remit to see hundreds of families in a year. In order to meet these demands, they adopted a Brief Therapy approach. Social workers, who became aware of the project's success with clients, developed – in partnership with them – a model designed to bring brief therapy principles and methods into child protection work. Their approach offers a structure to facilitate the integration of family *and* professional knowledge, from intake through to closure. They see partnership and paternalism as being on a continuum.

> *Partnership exists when both the statutory agency and the family cooperate and make efforts to achieve specific, mutually understood goals. Partnership cannot be categorised by an equitable distribution of power between family and agency. One demonstration of this is the fact that the agency will almost always begin the relationship and necessarily defines when it will conclude.*
>
> *(Turnell and Edwards 1999)*

It is not possible or appropriate to outline the approach here in all its detail or to describe 'how to do it'. In the case of the collaboration in Perth (Australia) a full programme of training took place with the social workers involved. But within the approach are a series of practice principles and a form to aid assessment, which can be useful to those social workers concerned with issues of partnership and ensuring they assess safety as well as danger.

Practice principles

The following is a précis of the Practice principles that form a backdrop to the assessments, as described by Turnell and Edwards (1999).

Practice principles that build partnerships

1. **Respect service recipients as people worth doing business with (not *to*)**
   This is not to be confused with naïve practice, a fear of challenging or a rule of optimism.

2. **Cooperate with the person not the abuse**
   This involves acknowledging strengths as well as weaknesses and not treating individuals as 'another job lot'. This includes showing awareness and sensitivity about the stress brought on by the assessment process or investigation itself.

3. **Recognise that cooperation is possible even where coercion is required**
   The authors stress the importance of recognising inequality of power but using it sensitively in a 'considered and skilful fashion'.

4. **Recognise that all families have signs of safety**
   Families are often 'pigeon-holed' and seen primarily in the context of their 'problem' label and this is not weighed up with other aspects of their behaviour and being.

5. **Maintain a focus on safety**
   The Signs of safety approach suggests focusing on goals and talking about 'presence' rather than 'absence', for example telling the mother of a neglected child that she needs to be in earshot and eyesight of the baby at all times.

6. **Learn what the service recipient wants**
   This refers to the importance of harnessing the motivations of service users. For example, the client might not agree with the social workers' concerns but might be motivated by wanting the worker 'out of his or her hair' and be willing to make changes for that end which might fit with the workers' explicitly safety-focused goals.

7. **Always search for detail**
   The authors stress the importance of obtaining detailed and balanced information – that is, thorough, negative and positive, from sources inside and outside the family. This serves as an antidote to naïve practice and provides the best basis for realistic assessment and case plans. Also, thorough exploration will increase the chances of identifying antecedents, consequences, patterns, feelings and opportunities for change.

8. **Focus on creating small change**
   The tradition of Brief Therapy holds that change is continuous and therefore one (small) change will inevitably lead to further change. Frequently, trying to achieve big goals quickly leads to frustration. A focus on specific, small changes can be more useful, even if only for the reason that people have a sense of something being achieved.

9. **Don't confuse case details with judgements**
   This approach stresses the difference between an event and the value or meaning ascribed to it. For example, if a mother walks out of a meeting she could be labelled as uncooperative and future information might be used to 'prove' this further; when in fact she had had a terrible week, was being asked questions she'd answered many times before, and had a view (perhaps founded) that those present had already 'made up their minds'.

10. **Offer choices**

Where possible, the likelihood of a family engaging constructively with a process is heightened by having choices to minimise (but not eradicate) the power differential. The worker needs to be clear about the non-negotiable aspects of the case however, for example, 'We need to discuss these issues with you today. Can you suggest the best time and place for us to meet during the day?'

11. **Treat the interview as a forum for change**

The interview is the intervention – the authors argue that even child protection investigations can be therapeutic. The investigations can develop a family's understanding of issues and offer support and education. The case plan and interventions are the 'icing on the cake'. The interview is the relationship between worker and family and is the principal vehicle for change.

Finally, we are reminded to treat the practice principles as aspirations rather than assuming that, because the worker agrees with them in theory, they are being adhered to.

Practice elements

In addition to the Practice principles outlined above, Turnell and Edwards listed the following *Six practice elements*, which attempt to translate the principles into practice behaviours or values that should guide social workers' responses and actions in the assessment process.

The following is a précis of the practice elements described by Turnell and Edwards (1999).

1. **Understand the position of each family member**

This includes their position in relation to the problem, the solution, and the statutory agency. For example: regarding the problem *(I was hit as a child and it never did me any harm)*; the solution *(I don't need to talk, I just need some practical help)*; and the statutory agency *(If I tell them the truth they'll take my child away)*. A person's position includes their strongly held values, beliefs and the meanings they attach to things. Once the social worker *thinks* they have established the position of the person, they should always repeat it back to them to check this out.

The authors liken understanding the position to understanding the plot in a play. Once you 'get' the characters, the plot and their actions make more sense.

2. **Exceptions to the neglect**

'Exception questions' can be useful in eliciting information. For example: 'Tell me about the times when you get your child to listen to you without shouting at her.' This question is based on two assumptions: that the problem is not happening all the time; and that the person probably deals appropriately with the problem some of the time. Questioning such as this can uncover the absence of neglectful behaviour as well as the presence of safe and constructive behaviours. It is important to explore the details, asking the *how, when, where* and *what* of the incident; and to find out how confident the person is in their ability to repeat the exception.

Exception questions can be useful at referral stage and beyond. For example: 'Can you tell me about times when (the parent) has responded appropriately in keeping the child safe? What did she do?' A positive answer will perhaps provide a way forward when meeting with the parent, and a negative one may alert the social worker to a potentially malicious referrer.

In training, the authors suggest asking the question three times before deciding there is no answer – start by recognising that you [the social worker] are changing emphasis/shifting conversation, and only move on to exception questions after you have fully acknowledged what is being said about the problem or incident.

3. **Family strengths and resources**
   Michael White (1988) in Turnell and Edwards (1999) said that 'problem saturated description(s)' lead to impotence and hopelessness, which frequently happens to all concerned in child protection. By seeking to expand on this picture we can acknowledge some foundations on which to build the families' strengths. Once again the answers to questions regarding strengths and resources can generate positive and constructive information and/or someone's inability to see anything positively can be highlighted.

Example question

We have been talking about some very serious matters. To give me a more balanced picture, can you tell me some of the things that you feel are good about this family?

4. **Focus on goals**
   Weick (1989, in Turnell and Edwards 1999) said: *The question is not what kind of life one has had but what kind of life one wants and then bringing to bear all the personal and social resources available to accomplish this goal.*

   Careful and explicit emphasis on the goals of both family and agency are the foundation of this approach, but the authors argue it is perhaps one of the most difficult to achieve and requires detailed knowledge of the case and careful thinking.

Examples of questions to elicit a family's safety goals

For our involvement with your family to be useful to you, what would need to happen? What would change in your family? What would change about your partner/your child?

The authors argue that, whilst the level of overlap between the goals of family member and those of professionals can vary greatly – and at times be hard to find – it is often possible to explore safety without complete agreement about the abuse or neglect. The goals should be firmed up ('concretised'), with specific, measurable steps identified towards achieving the necessary change.

5. **Scaling safety and progress**
   By using scaling questions, workers can obtain information that is specific and detailed. This approach can be particularly useful with children.

Example of a scaling question

On a scale of 0–10, where 10 would mean things in this family are just the way you want them, and 0, that life could not be worse – where would you rate your family right now?

This approach is simple, direct, and easy to understand. Also, it calls for a very precise assessment of the situation from the service user – turning the paternalistic model of social worker as expert on its head. The approach often evokes very significant information.

This type of questioning has been criticised for putting too much onus on the family, or child, to assess their own situation; but it is only a tool, and information is not necessarily taken at face value. One woman, for example, rated her life a '4'; but when questioned about what positive things brought it up to a '4', she broke down and said it was really a '0' and began to admit and discuss in detail how depressed she had been feeling.

6. **Willingness, confidence and capacity**

For any plan to work with a family, consideration needs to be given to their engagement with it; their willingness, confidence and capacity to achieve it.

Examples of scaling questions to assess each of these areas

Willingness

Ask: *If I asked you to do_____, on a scale of 0–10, how willing would you be?*
Then: *What, if anything, would increase your willingness to do something about these problems?*

Capacity to take action

Ask: *On a scale of 0–10, how would you rate your ability to do something about these problems?*

Then: *What parts of these plans would you feel most able to try? What or who could help you do these things?*

Confidence

On a scale of 0–10, how confident are you that you (your family) can do things to make your child safer (stop the abuse)? What would increase your confidence?

There is a case example in the book about a concerned grandmother, who seemed to point all problems to her son-in-law (stepfather) until scaling questions revealed her concerns would only shift half a point if he were to be out of the family.

Finally, the Signs of safety approach provides a useful form – with a scale for safety and progress – on which to record the relative safety and danger as the social worker sees it during their assessment of a family. In practice, the form is designed to be used where the principles described have already influenced the work that has taken place. However, social workers who were unfamiliar with the principles prior to their participation on the Putting analysis into assessment project, were able in many cases to utilise the form straight away, applying it to assessments they were undertaking and their feedback was often positive.

Practice tool 6: Signs of safety assessment and planning form

Signs of safety assessment and planning form

You may wish to spatially locate items between the danger and safety poles along this continuum.

Danger

List of all aspects that demonstrate likelihood of maltreatment (past, present or future)

Safety

List of all aspects that indicate safety (e.g. exceptions, strengths and resources, goals, willingness)

Safety and context scale

> Safety scale: Given the danger and safety information, rate the situation on a scale of 0–10, where 0 means recurrence of similar or worse abuse/neglect is certain and 10 means that there is sufficient safety for the child for you to close the case.
>
> Context scale: Rate this case on a scale of 0–10, where 10 means that this is not a situation where any action would be taken and 0 means this is the worst case of child abuse or neglect that the agency has seen.

Agency goals. What will the agency need to occur to be willing to close this case?

Family goals. What does the family want generally, and regarding safety?

Immediate progress. What would indicate to the agency that some small progress has been made?

Copyright © 1997 Steve Edwards and Andrew Turnell

Case study: Signs of safety

Name	Age	Gender	Ethnicity	Relationship
Kayleigh Bell	11 months	female	Mixed Parentage	subject (White British/Black Caribbean)
Sophie Cousins	5 years	female	White British	half-sister
Darren Cousins	9 years	male	White British	half-brother
Danielle Cousins	25 years	female	White British	mother
Frank Cousins	41 years	male	White British	father of Darren and Sophie
Jared Bell	29 years	male	Black Caribbean	Kayleigh's father

Kayleigh Bell is referred to the duty social worker by the ward sister on the paediatric ward at the General Hospital. She was admitted earlier that day after Danielle took her to the GP because she was unwell with diarrhoea and sickness.

Kayleigh was found by the GP to be dehydrated and underweight for her age and stage of development. She appeared grubby, her nappy appeared not to have been changed for a long time and she had severe nappy rash. She was inappropriately dressed for the cold weather, listless and weak. She has been put on emergency rehydration/nutritional therapy and is undergoing further tests.

During the admission examination, the registrar discovered old bruising on her ribs and the tops of her legs for which there was no obvious explanation. The registrar thought from their appearance that they might be non-accidental in cause.

The registrar and ward sister tried talking to Danielle about Kayleigh's general health and about the bruising. The ward sister described Danielle as seeming very low, flat and unresponsive. However, Danielle did say that Kayleigh had never been a settled baby, had been sickly throughout her life and had developed diarrhoea recently as well. The registrar thought that Danielle appeared depressed and somewhat confused. Danielle did not reportedly know how the bruises might have been caused.

Darren and Sophie attended hospital with their mother. Sophie appeared to be fairly well nourished but grubby, unkempt and rather 'out of control'. Darren seemed to be trying to take charge of the situation: trying to control Sophie's behaviour by shouting at her; and holding his mother's arm – guiding her as though she was unwell. He tried to answer some of the questions that the registrar was asking. He said that his mum had been unwell and that he'd been making the baby's feed and feeding her for the last two weeks.

The family only moved to the area two weeks ago from a neighbouring borough where they had been known to Social Services. An Initial Assessment was carried out there about four months ago after Darren and Sophie's school had referred them due to Darren's poor school attendance, his tiredness, grubbiness, generally anxious demeanour and Sophie's disruptive behaviour in the school nursery. The assessment had identified that Danielle seemed depressed and that the family were in need of support. They had been referred to a local NCH project but they had moved out of the area just as a place became available.

The family was also known by the neighbouring authority from a few years prior to that, as there had been several reports to the police about domestic violence by Frank Cousins who had lived in the family at the time. The family had been visited at the time by Social Services but Frank Cousins had by this time moved out and no further action was taken.

Kayleigh's father, Jared, was apparently living with the family until six months ago when he returned to London, his home city. Danielle told the ward sister that she hadn't seen him for about four months.

Figure 3.2 An example of a completed Signs of safety form (in relation to Case Study: Signs of safety)

Signs of safety assessment and planning form

You may wish to spatially locate items between the danger and safety poles along this continuum.

Danger

List of all aspects that demonstrate likelihood of maltreatment (past, present or future)

Sophie's behaviour

Current ill-health of child   Coping in-between referrals?

Underweight   Jared?

Grubby/unkempt

Nappy rash severe

Bruising

Unresponsiveness/low mood   Whilst providing some support to his mother Darren
No explanation for bruises   is taking responsibilities beyond his years & inadequate for baby.

Safety

List of all aspects that indicate safety (e.g. exceptions, strengths and resources, goals, willingness)

Cooperating with hospital   Danielle took child to GP

Danielle has shown willingness previously to accept help and background info from her
previous borough – suggests she acknowledged that she was feeling depressed.

Danielle has registered with a GP within 2 weeks of moving

Safety and context scale

Safety scale: Given the danger and safety information, rate the situation on a scale of 0–10, where 0 means recurrence of similar or worse
abuse/neglect is certain and 10 means that there is sufficient safety for the child for you to close the case.   5

Context scale: Rate this case on a scale of 0–10, where 10 means that this is not a situation where any action would be taken and 0 means
this is the worst case of child abuse or neglect that the agency has seen.   4

Agency goals. What will the agency need to occur to be willing to close this case?

Kayleigh's physical care needs being met (able to be met) consistently and adequately.
Acknowledgement by Danielle of seriousness of concerns and concrete plans to address this.
Alleviation of concern re. bruising?

Family goals. What does the family want generally, and regarding safety?

Washing machine to help in dressing children appropriately.
Home to be organised – post move is in disarray.
Resume and continue contact with Jared.
Support in dealing with ex-partner who's recently become involved.

Immediate progress. What would indicate to the agency that some small progress has been made?

Danielle receiving support in her own right for depression – to visit GP about this.
Recovery of Kayleigh.
Home conditions resolved.
Agreement to referral to family centre for parenting support.
Acknowledgement of concerns for Darren and Sophie.

Copyright © 1997 Steve Edwards and Andrew Turnell

Six practice elements

In working with this family, considerations could be given to applying the six practice elements. Examples of how the practice elements could relate to Case study: Signs of safety are given below.

1. *Understanding the position of each family member*   Danielle tends to feel guilty and 'like a failure' when she becomes depressed and is struggling to cope. For this reason she has been reluctant to ask for help even though she has found life harder since she and Jared split up. She is not unwilling to accept help and would welcome it, but is slow to recognise that her depression affects her ability to judge what she needs. Darren views himself as the 'man of the house' and has been keen to look after his mother and siblings and reluctant to talk about his situation to anyone in case they 'interfere'. He has been struggling to look after Kayleigh and has always identified with his father and wondered if there is something wrong with him because his father was violent towards his mother.

2. *Exceptions to the neglect*   It would be useful to explore with Danielle and the children how things have been previously. The previous involvement with the neighbouring borough would suggest that between Frank leaving the family home and the most recent referral, the family coped without social services hearing of any concerns from school or health visitors. This would indicate that Danielle might have been managing adequately during that time. One might ask Danielle, for example: 'Can you tell me about a time when you have felt happier and been proud of the way you have looked after the children?' Or Sophie could be asked about her achievements or when adults have praised her to counter the picture of her being 'out of control'.

3. *Family strengths and resources*   Despite her depression and having only moved into the area two weeks ago, Danielle has managed to recognise the urgency of Kayleigh's condition and organised an emergency GP appointment. She has also shown a willingness, through the previous assessment, to accept support. Jared could possibly be a useful source of support to the family if arrangements were made; and Darren has shown a level of care and closeness in his behaviour towards his mother and sisters.

4. *Focus on goals*   The difficulty that Danielle is having in meeting the basic care needs of her children have been compounded by the recent house move and her depression. There could well be some overlap between what she and the agency want; if, for example, Danielle wants the house to be organised, things unpacked and the washing machine plumbed in. She probably wants to feel better in herself, too, and to have more energy for the children. If Danielle was clear that she wanted Kayleigh home from hospital as soon as possible, this too would give common ground and a way forward for professionals to establish with her what would need to happen for this to take place.

5. *Scaling safety and progress*   Scaling questions could provide a sense of Danielle's feelings over time. She could be asked to rate where she is now and then at previous times in her mood. She could also be asked what it would take for her to move up the scale a couple of notches. Similarly, Sophie and Darren could be asked about their views in this way, for example: 'If 10 is wonderful and 1 is terrible, how do you feel about living in your new house?' This could be built on, with questions arising from the response to ascertain what would make the difference, and how the situation now differs from the last house or when Jared lived in the home.

6. *Willingness, confidence and capacity*   It would be very important to explore how committed, able and confident Danielle is to carry out any plans that emerge, as her low mood could lead to her agreeing passively to things but not in a meaningful way. Similarly, her lack of confidence and tendency to think she is a 'bad parent' could undermine her efforts. Specific questions about these areas, could include: 'On a scale of 1–10, how confident are you that you can keep this up (improvements in practical care of Kayleigh)?' and 'What would increase your confidence?'

Some of these points may seem rather obvious and, of course, any considerations of safety factors and strengths would be weighed up alongside the fairly serious concerns that have arisen about Kayleigh, taking into account the established, or suspected, cause of her bruises. However, active pursuit of shared goals and strengths may increase the chances of a successful intervention.

Practice development session 6: The signs of safety approach

Aim

To introduce the Signs of safety approach; and to consider and test out how it might be usefully applied to practice and contribute to analysis and decision-making.

Method

- Give a presentation to the participants on the Signs of safety approach, outlining its main messages and potential applications, using Presentation 6 slides 50–56. Download from www.ncb.org.uk/resources/support).

- Distribute the Six practice elements (page 63), to the participants.

- Invite participants to form six groups or pairs.

- Give each group or pair a different practice element to focus on.

- Tell them to read the relevant part of the handout and plan a brief five-minute presentation, to be given to the wider group, in which they will convey what the practice element is and give examples of how it may be applied in their work.

- When the planning is complete, reconvene the full group, then invite each group or pair in turn to give their presentation.

- Distribute the Signs of safety assessment and planning form (page 66).

- Run through the key elements of the form. Then invite participants to work, either individually or in small groups, on completing the form in relation to a real case they are involved with. If this is not possible, tell them to use Case study: Signs of safety instead (page 67). There are, of course, no right answers.

Involving children

This section explores some of the issues that arise when practitioners are trying to incorporate and provide a balanced assessment of the views and perceptions of children within an analysis. It is widely accepted that enabling children's participation in matters that affect them is essential to good practice. The UN Convention on the Rights of the Child, ratified by the UK government in 1991, recognises children's rights to express their views freely in all matters affecting them and for their views to be given 'due weight in accordance with the age and maturity of the child'. The importance of ascertaining and responding to children's views is enshrined further in the Human Rights Act 1998 and the Children Act 1989.

In the context of assessing the needs of children, gaining an understanding of their perspective in relation to their own situation and lives is essential to meeting their needs and protecting them. An assessment is incomplete without a child's perspective, which is a key source of information. It is not enough to consider how the child appears to present to professionals, referrers or family members – although this information is also valuable and important – because the way a child appears on the outside will not necessarily point clearly to what they are thinking, feeling or experiencing. Signs and symptoms of abuse or neglect are difficult to identify as the behaviour and apparent mood of a child or young person may vary over time and have a range of explanations.

However, whilst few would argue with the importance of obtaining and considering children's views, time and again research and case reviews indicate that we are falling short in this area. Ofsted's 2010 review of lessons from serious case reviews highlighted five main messages, summarised in Munro 2011 as follows:

- child was not seen often enough by professionals, or not asked about their views and feelings

- agencies didn't listen to adults who tried to speak on the child's behalf and had important information to contribute

- parents and carers prevented professionals from seeing and listening to the child

- practitioners focused too much on parents' needs, especially vulnerable parents and overlooked the implications of the child

- agencies did not interpret their findings well enough to protect the child.

Furthermore, children and young people themselves have informed those undertaking consultations with them that in their experience social workers are not always good at listening to them or properly recording their wishes and feelings. In the consultation carried out by the Children's Rights Director for England (Morgan 2011), which informed the Munro review, fewer than a quarter of children who were looked after thought that their wishes and feelings had made some or a lot of difference to the decision to take them into care, while 67 per cent thought their wishes had definitely not made a difference. In relation to their ongoing relationship with social workers, 50 per cent thought the worker didn't usually take notice of their wishes and feelings. The feedback is not all bad though. Research carried out by Action for Children for a review by C4EO (2010) found children to be overwhelmingly positive about their social workers, but it is clear that professionals struggle overall to form and maintain effective and trusting relationships with children within the context of all assessments affecting them.

We will consider what helps professionals communicate effectively with children, but first it may be helpful to consider what the potential barriers are.

Barriers for children

Children themselves may have a number of reasons for not wanting to disclose their feelings or wishes. C4EO (2010) in their review of children's experiences of the protection/safeguarding system list a range of barriers to telling that have been identified in studies (Mariathasan, Featherstone, Garvey and others, Stein, Nelson, Toompsett and others, Cawson, the Scottish Executive, Get Connected, all in C4EO (2010):

- lack of awareness that the behaviour was abusive

- shame, embarrassment and self-blame

- stigma, loss of credibility, friends finding out

- the fear of loss of control and of people taking over

- getting someone else into trouble or splitting the family up

- loyalty for or feeling sorry for the abuser

- access to someone to tell, not knowing where to go for help

- concerns about confidentiality

- concerns about whether the person is competent to deal with the issue

- fear that telling will make things worse and that the abuser will be told that they have disclosed

- not being able to express oneself

- believing in self-reliance, not wishing to burden others.

Barriers for professionals

With so many factors affecting children's likelihood of feeling able to tell professionals about their experiences or views, it is even more important that professionals have the necessary skills and approaches to try and overcome this. However, there are barriers to this as well. The pressures of working with vulnerable parents can often divert attention away from children (Brandon and others 2008 and 2009) and many practitioners have reported feeling ill equipped to communicate with children particularly given the diverse range of ages, abilities and needs they encounter among the children they work with. Time is also an important factor. It takes time to build trusting relationships and to get to know children well enough to understand what things mean to them. Professionals frequently report that they simply do not have enough time to spend undertaking direct work with children and their families. Munro (2011) highlighted how an increase in 'proceduralisation' in recent years has reduced the time social workers had to spend directly with children and families.

What helps?

In seeking to understand how best to overcome the barriers to involving children effectively in assessments or at least how best to maximise the effectiveness of what can be done within the constraints of professional roles, it is helpful to consider what children and young people say they find helpful. In the consultation carried out by the Children's Rights Director of England, the young people said that the best way for professionals to find out their wishes and feelings was to ask them on their own, face-to-face. They wanted to be given real choices and for workers to ensure that when they offered them choices they have the information they needed and felt free to state their true feelings.

> They shouldn't ask in front of your mum if you want your mum to be there at the interview. What can you say?

> (Nelson cited in C4EO 2010)

They wanted a choice of venues including the option of somewhere neutral (not school or home) and some commented that they did not want formal rooms with tables in them and found it off putting if workers had lots of paperwork with them. They wanted ongoing relationships and continuity of worker and for them to be easily accessible.

When Action for Children undertook a consultation for C4EO (2010) they explored the helpful things that social workers did. Answers included: talking and listening (including giving explanations, being calm and having an informal manner), keeping in touch, helping to sort out problems, getting them involved in activities, being positive and fun ('they should not be too serious or formal, not be a wet blanket or too boring'), getting on with the serious and important things ('he tackles the problem bit by bit so it will get done'), and helping them with their behaviour. Other studies have found children deemed the following qualities to be important in social workers:

caring, understanding, knowledgeable, hard-working, trustworthy and available, offering advice and suggestions without forcing opinions on them, accessible, sticking with them over time and culturally competent (C4EO 2010, drawing on Wiffin (2010), Nelson (2008), Humphreys and others (2008), Bennett and White (2004), Mainey and others (2009), Tunnard (2004)).

The information given to children to help them understand the process of assessments, including what might happen in the future has been explored too. Mainey and others (2009) highlighted that when they are anxious, children might not be able to remember or understand the information given to them and young people have suggested that information be given to them 'verbally and in writing and repeated after the upheaval'. It helps if workers are not only clear with children and young people about why they want to see them and what might happen when they do meet, but also if workers show empathy, interest and understanding in the child's fears about sharing information.

> She said to me, what's your experience of social workers? That helped me. She encouraged me to tell the bad things as well as the good.

> *(Wiffin 2010)*

Children have also highlighted the importance of being able to trust professionals whom they share their thoughts and feelings with. This is helped by professionals being honest with them, reliable and doing what they say they will do.

Children also commented on the importance of professionals considering the effect of the situation on all family members when they are working with one child and the family or the parents.

> Our worker would boss my mum and dad around. Not explaining, but telling them. It felt weird to have them undermined. It was confusing to me that they weren't in charge anymore.

> My sister confides in me. She wouldn't tell the social worker stuff that she would tell me so I could say things on her behalf. The social worker didn't like this ... she wanted her to say it ... they should be open to listen to what other people in the family might say on their behalf.

It also emerged in the consultation for the Munro review that where decisions affected all the children in a family, it was often only the older siblings who were asked their views. This might reflect a lack of confidence or skill in communicating with younger children. The children consulted thought that very young children would find it easier to communicate if they had toys to play with while things were explained to them. In fact older children too said it was helpful to have something to distract you while you were talking such as something to fiddle with or squeeze or being able to draw or make something at the same time as having a conversation. For younger children, drawing and writing were thought to be helpful and possibly having someone they trusted already in the room. Most importantly they said the child needed to feel comfortable, but what this would entail would depend on the individual child.

Children and young people also said they wanted a range of ways to be able to communicate, including written or video diaries, SMS texts and emails. Being creative and receptive to what children and young people's preferences are is also likely to enhance communication with adolescents (Brandon and others 2008, 2009 study of serious case reviews showed adolescents to be vulnerable to suicide and self-harm when living within abusive and neglectful circumstances). Establishing children's preferences is also particularly important when working with disabled children. Even where the child's method of communication is through a sign or symbol system such as Makaton, it might help the child feel that they are valued by professionals if they try to learn at least some basic skills in the child's method for use in conjunction with facilitators when required. It also helps to assume that children are competent and to focus and build on what they can do rather than what they can't.

In addition to the messages above from children and young people, research has also demonstrated the importance of the initial response to a child who is trying to share a concern with an adult (Prior, Lynch and Glaser, 1994). They may only try once to tell someone something that is worrying them or happening to them and it is important that the adult conveys a willingness to listen and shows interest in what the child has to say, without cross-examining them. Some children have reported that they felt they were not believed when they were interviewed in the context of child protection investigations (Nelson, Westcott, Woolfson in C4EO 2010) and Woolfson suggests explaining to children that 'questioning their account for the purposes of clarity or evidence, does not indicate disbelief'.

It is important that professionals notice changes in children's behaviour and if it concerns them, show their concern to a child, asking them to explain the change. Jones and others (2006) suggests a range of factors to support professionals in approaching communication with children, including the following:

- maintaining personal neutrality about any issues raised (but not indifference)

- managing one's personal responses to any distressing material that the child communicates

- seeing the child or young person as the expert, not the adult practitioner

- convey genuine empathic concern, to a degree that is congruent with the situation

- using open-ended and unbiased approaches to communication and allowing the child to recall their experiences freely

- bearing in mind that if the adult does not ask, it is unlikely that the child will tell

- recording the exchange in detail, including its content and duration

- clarifying any ambiguous information arising from the child or any other adult.

How do children's contributions inform the analysis?

Even where efforts are made to establish the perspective of the child in an assessment, it can still be a challenge for professionals to weigh and balanced information they obtain from children. Also it needs to be acknowledged that inevitably the social worker's knowledge of how the child experiences and views things will be partial and based on information that only represents the child at one point in time. This is not a criticism, but often a reality and, if the analysis of a child's situation and needs is to be fair and balanced, this needs to be acknowledged and of course addressed as far as possible. Consulting widely with others who know the child well; observing the child and receiving information on others' observations in a wide variety of settings over time; doing all that one possibly can to find out about the child; and trying to ensure they do have someone trustworthy and accessible to express their views to, can all help to address the partiality of the picture we have of the child.

However, all too often, social workers fail to acknowledge the limitations of their knowledge about what is happening in families generally and, in particular, with regard to the views of the child. This was often borne out in the Putting analysis into assessment project when assessment reports were read out, either generally or for audit. It was often unclear in the reports to what extent the author had got to know the child; and what level of contact with, and knowledge of, the child the comments were based upon. The evidence regarding the situation of the child and their family and about the quality of parenting itself was often very descriptive and spoke for itself, but there was less clarity when it came to representing children.

Whilst there was usually some attempt to describe children's views, either through what they had said or their presenting behaviour, it was often hard to put this into context. Many of the reports would have benefited from some further discussion of the extent to which the child's views had been elicited so far. In contrast, parents' views and perceptions usually made up the main body of the reports.

Sally Holland in her book *Child and Family Assessment in Social Work Practice* (2004) describes similar findings in the study she conducted between 1997 and 2001. She closely examined casework within two neighbouring coastal cities and found that much of the focus in assessments was on establishing the 'verbal performance and ability to provide plausible explanations' for the family problems of parents. Whilst this is necessary, children tended to be excluded or marginalised. Where children were described they were often 'minor characters' in the narrative of assessments, whilst parents were portrayed in a lively in-depth manner. For example in one 25-page report, there were eight pages of detailed description and analysis of the mother whereas the four children were portrayed in just two pages in total, the two-year-old in four sentences. This balancing of the information was not unusual. It was not just the quantity of information about children that was lacking, but the way in which they were described was often two-dimensional and partial.

So why is it so difficult for practitioners to do justice to the contribution children can make to the assessment? Apart from the difficulties in building the relationships with children – and the very real challenge due to their age, verbal and reasoning skills of finding out what they feel, want and have experienced – there is often ambivalence amongst social workers and others involved in assessment regarding how to make sense of and weight the information that children give. In the Putting analysis into assessment project, social workers spoke of the pressure they felt to be 'concrete'. They often did not feel sufficiently well-placed to make clear statements about the meanings of children's behaviour or what they said. There were often fairly general comments about attachment or a child's level of development in relation to what could be expected, but social workers told us that they worried about making these connections in too forthright a manner because they were not psychologists and they expected to be challenged by 'experts' in the court arena. In one local authority we worked with, the legal department discouraged social workers from referring to research and theory in their assessments for this reason. Holland (2004) noted in her study that social work assessments often referred in some way to the child's attachment; but that it was not explored usefully by putting it into context as to how the child was with people other than their parent, for example, or in other settings. She also found an overemphasis on comparing children to developmental norms, in some cases in an unhelpful and unbalanced way. This often resulted in objectifying children and, in some cases, children's names were inserted into text that replicated the language of development charts exactly. The following is one of Holland's examples of this.

> *Aran knows and immediately turns to his own name and babbles loudly and incessantly and imitates adults' playful vocalisation with gleeful enthusiasm.*

The use of evidence, research and theories – such as relating what is known to attachment theory or child development theories – is encouraged, and the *Framework for Assessment of Children in Need and their Families* (Department of Health and others 2000) is grounded in such knowledge, but references to it need to be clear and illustrative. Most importantly, Holland urges, we need to be 'thoughtful and critical' in our application of such knowledge given the potential for 'powerful arguments to be made by using a flawed or overly narrow evidence base'.

Another tendency reported by Holland (2004), and also experienced during the Putting analysis into assessment project, is to influence the reader's thinking about the child through the use of language. For example, if in the same sentence as saying that 'Charlotte has a vivid imagination and seems to take pleasure in getting her friends into trouble' we say that she has told us that she is being bullied, we are undermining what she has told us in quite an obvious way. Or similarly, if we are reporting that a child has been saying she misses her mother (as she is in foster care) but at the same time we say that the child says things only to please her mother, once again we are calling the child's view into question. It is fine to say all of the above things if we can illustrate them clearly with examples – but the ordering of points, the decisions about what we include and what we leave out of a report (verbal or written) are potentially loaded by our motivations in 'arguing a case' with an intended response in mind.

The challenge of representing children accurately and fairly is often increased when working with disabled children, or those whose verbal or non-verbal communication is not readily understood. It is of course essential to draw on all possible resources, creative communication techniques and equipment or facilitators where this may further our ability to ascertain a child's contribution to the assessment, but equally important is the need for the practitioner to acknowledge the gaps and limitations in their understanding. This makes them less likely to misrepresent a child through assumptions or partial information and more likely to identify where the child needs further opportunities to express their views.

It is crucial to remember that the most important thing to try and understand about and for the children and young people is how they are interpreting the things they are experiencing. Butler and Williamson (1994) highlighted the importance of not just knowing what a child's experiences were, but of understanding the meaning they attached to them. They cite an example of a girl whose father murdered her mother. For her, the fact of the murder was not what she identified as her worst experience, but the lack of communication and support that followed it. The authors found this to be the case with a vast range of experiences – ranging from the extreme to the 'everyday', such as arguments with siblings over a computer game – it was the meaning of the event that mattered. Similarly Holland (2004) cites Scott (1998) as finding, in an Australian study of assessments involving sexual abuse, that much of the focus tended to be on whether or not the case should be labelled as abuse; with assumptions being made about the child's feelings rather than exploring the key issue of 'how is the child?'

Finally, an exploration and presentation of a child's views and experiences should be approached holistically, finding out about the positive things in their lives, the things they enjoy, value and hope for in addition to the difficulties and concerns that they have.

During the Putting analysis into assessment project, an analysis tool on this subject was not used. However, the project did generate sufficient information – from exploring themes, reading reports and highlighting key issues – for a checklist to be compiled to assist practitioners and managers when considering the information they have in relation to a child. It can be usefully integrated into the practitioner's analysis.

Practice tool 7: Checklist for involving children in assessment

How well do you know the child and to what extent do you know their views, feelings and wishes?	This includes describing your relationship with them, how you think they perceive you, how often you have seen them and in what context – where and who else was present?
Which adults (including professionals) know the child best and what do they think the child's key concerns and views are?	What is their relationship like – how well-placed are they to represent the child's views?
What opportunities does the child have to express their views to trusted or 'safe' adults?	Does the child know how to access people, what would be the barriers and what has been done to ensure they know where to go if they want to talk to someone?
How (if at all) has the child defined the problems in their family/life and the effects the problems are having on them?	This includes the child's perceptions and fears; and what they themselves perceive as the primary causes of pain, distress and fear. What opportunities has the child had to explore them?
When the child has shared information, views or feelings, in what circumstances has this occurred and what if anything did they want to happen?	This should only be stated if known (can be clearly demonstrated). Assumptions should not be made about a child's motivations for communicating something.
What has been observed regarding the child's way of relating and responding to key adults, such as parents and foster carers? Does this raise concerns about attachment?	This would include describing any differences in the way the child presents with different people or in different contexts. And, where conclusions are being drawn about the child's attachment, the reasons for such conclusions should be clearly demonstrated.
What is your understanding of the research evidence in relation to the experiences this child is thought to have had, and how they might affect them? How far is what you know of this particular child consistent with the above?	What are the likely or possible impacts on children who experience (*the specific issue at hand, such as parental alcohol misuse, domestic violence*). This includes a consideration of potential harm along with resilience factors.
What communication methods have been employed in seeking the views and feelings of the child; and to what extent have these optimised the child's opportunity to contribute their views?	This includes considerations of whether equipment, facilitators, interpreters, the use of signs or symbols, play, and storybooks could be helpful and whether the child's preferences are known.
How confident are you that you have been able to establish the child's views, wishes and feelings as far as is reasonable and possible for the child? How much sense are you able to make of the information you do have?	This would include considerations of things that may have hindered such communication, such as pressure from other adults, time limitations, language barriers or lack of trust in the child–social worker relationship.

Case study: Involving children

Kelly	(subject)	8 years old
Susan	(mother)	32 years old
Jim	(father)	31 years old (lives separately but locally)

Kelly has recently come to the attention of social services in the local area. The neighbouring social services were involved with her on two occasions in the past: once in relation to setting up a place in an after-school club for her – this was undertaken by the disabled children's team as Kelly was thought to have mild learning difficulties and behavioural difficulties; and once when a duty visit was undertaken after a neighbour had reported that Kelly had been left home alone. Both parents denied that this had occurred.

Recently, your department has become involved because you have been contacted by Susan's mother requesting help for Susan in managing Kelly's needs. Susan has physical disabilities and is a wheelchair user; and Jim has recently moved out following an argument with Susan to which the police were called to attend.

A few visits have been undertaken by yourself and other duty social workers since the referral was made and, on these visits, it has been observed that the hygiene levels in the home are poor. The kitchen, lounge and Kelly's room are fairly tidy but in need of a clean and you are aware that Susan's mother visited days ago and said she had cleared up, but Susan's bedroom is very dirty, with beer cans, dirty tissue, used sanitary wear and dirty laundry littering the floor and under the bed. Susan says that Jim was drinking a lot before he left the home and stopped cleaning up a long time ago. Susan is tearful when you meet with her and acknowledges the problems but only when they are pointed out to her.

Carers have been going into the home to help with practical tasks recently and they have raised concerns with their supervisor about what one carer described as Kelly's 'wild' behaviour. She kicks and screams if she doesn't get her own way and tells them she will call the police on them and 'get them arrested for child abuse' when they try and supervise her. Susan is eager to keep Kelly at home and is passive and fairly unresponsive when the concerns about Kelly are raised with her. She starts telling you and the carers who visit that Jim was sometimes aggressive towards her, that he neglected her and Kelly and drank too much. She says she did not tell anyone before because she didn't want people interfering. Initially she did not want Jim to return to the home, but lately she is tearful and missing him, saying that they have spoken on the phone and she hopes he will return.

Susan's mother has just contacted you to say that she is sure (though Susan is denying it) that Jim moved back in on the previous weekend. Kelly's school are describing her as 'very high' and quite 'destructive' in the past few days but stress that her behaviour has been a concern for a long time and she rarely talks about home.

What conclusions can we draw from Kelly's contribution to this assessment so far? Below are some examples of the sorts of points that could be elicited from the checklist headings in relation to this case scenario.

1) How well do you know the child and to what extent do you know their views, feelings and wishes?	The social worker has only known Kelly for a few weeks and seen her, so far, on two occasions. At this stage only an initial assessment has been completed and whilst the social worker has a sense of how Kelly presents in school, after-school club and with her mother, there is a need to more fully explore her views and wishes. Her recent behaviour would suggest that she is unsettled at the moment.
2) Which adults [including professional(s)] know the child best; and what do they think the child's key concerns and views are?	Whilst the carers in the home have the most recent insight into what has been happening to Kelly of late, they have not been involved for long or consistently and their primary role is to give Susan practical support. Kelly has had a consistently good relationship with her teacher, Mrs Morris; and has told the social worker that she likes Rose, the escort on her school bus. Both Mrs Morris and Rose are concerned that Kelly's behaviour has recently been more erratic than usual and that she is seeking more attention through challenging behaviour, but when she gets it is resistant and hostile. They both think Kelly is feeling anxious and unsettled at the moment although they do not know whether or not she would prefer her Dad to come home. She rarely talks about home usually.
3) What opportunities does the child have to express their views to trusted or 'safe' adults?	Although Kelly has some fairly positive relationships with school staff, the escort, and one helper in particular at the after-school club, she usually sees them in group contexts with several other young people. Recently, because people are aware that Kelly is having a difficult time, her teacher and escort have been trying to give her some one-to-one time, which seems to have calmed her down at the time. Susan has acknowledged that she has been upset and preoccupied recently, but has agreed to try and ensure Kelly knows she can talk to her about how she is feeling.
4) How (if at all) has the child defined the problems in their family/life and the effects the problems are having on them?	At this stage Kelly has not explicitly talked about her situation, except for when her helper at the after-school club enquired (because Kelly was picked up by a carer instead of her dad). About this, Kelly said 'He's gone off in a strop hasn't he?'
5) When the child has shared information, views or feelings, in what circumstances has this occurred and what if anything did they want to happen?	When the social worker tried to talk with Kelly about the fact that her dad has moved out and suggested it must feel different at home, Kelly shrugged and asked 'Is he coming back?' in a fairly flat voice. When the social worker told her she doesn't know, Kelly changed the subject instantly, asking the social worker to go into the garden with her before running off outside to see the neighbour's 10-year-old boy.
6) What has been observed regarding the child's way of relating and responding to key adults, such as parents and foster carers? Does this raise concerns about attachment?	In the first visit to the home, Kelly was observed to be extremely active, running around, slamming doors and clambering all over the social worker, even though it was the first time of meeting her. She appeared to pay no attention to Susan's attempts at supervising her and was fairly aggressive towards her; swinging her bag around her head so it hit her mother despite being told to stop, and digging her nails into Susan when Susan tried to stop her running off.

7) What is your understanding of the research evidence in relation to the experiences this child is thought to have had, and how they might affect them? How far is what you know of this particular child consistent with the above?	There has been some suggestion by Susan and also highlighted by the recent police attendance at the home, that Kelly has certainly been present when conflicts have taken place between her parents in the form of heated arguments and has possibly witnessed domestic violence. Also, the beer cans, along with claims by Susan and her mother that Jim was drinking heavily in the months preceding his departure, suggest she has experienced seeing her father (and possibly Susan – according to the neighbour) drunk at home on a number of occasions. Both domestic violence and parental drinking are known to increase the likelihood of children of Kelly's age experiencing anxiety, being drawn into conflicts and taking sides with one parent; and of either internalising their feelings and experiencing anxiety or externalising them and presenting with challenging behaviour.
8) What communication methods have been employed in seeking the views and feelings of the child; and to what extent have these optimised the child's opportunity to contribute their views?	Kelly has good verbal communication skills and, in relation to other areas of her life (e.g. school, friendships), tends to make her feelings known to adults around her. Kelly does seem to become most chatty when engaged in imaginative play and in one-to-one situations. The social worker is planning to make some more time available for doing direct work with Kelly to get to know her better. Other professionals involved are trying to make themselves more accessible.
9) How confident are you that you have been able to establish the child's views, wishes and feelings as far as is reasonable and possible for the child? How much sense are you able to make of the information you do have?	Kelly's views about her situation are unclear, but it is obviously not ideal for her to be looked after by a succession of carers with little consistency; and her behaviour recently may be a reaction to this, as well as to her father's sudden departure from the home. It seems, from what Susan and other professionals have said to the social worker, that Kelly has shown signs of being unsettled for some time and the aggressive and challenging behaviour is not new or unusual for her but is more extreme. The understanding of her views, wishes and feelings at this stage is only partial.

Practice development session 7: Involving children

Three separate activities are detailed below for use in practice development sessions and training. These can be handpicked or combined depending on the needs of the group and time available.

Activity 1

Aim

To remind participants of the importance of being critical and thorough in relation to the information provided to them by and about children and young people in order to ensure balanced and fair analysis in relation to them.

Method

- Give a presentation on the issues to consider when analysing the information children give us. Presentation 7 slides 58-76 or distribute the section on involving children (pages 71 to 77) for participants to read.

- Invite discussion on the issues involved.

- Distribute the Practice tool, Checklist for involving children in assessment (page 78) to all the participants.

- Ask participants to each call to mind a child who they are, or have been, involved with through their work.

- Invite the participants to form pairs.

- Encourage the participants, in their pairs, to take it in turns to run through the checklist identifying what significant information they do know about the child and where the gaps are.

- When they seem to have completed this exercise, ask the pairs in turn to give feedback to the full group on how this went. If necessary, prompt them with questions such as: Did the checklist elicit more information or different information than you might otherwise have provided in an assessment or court report? Do you see any difficulties with either accessing or reporting on some of the information the checklist elicited?

Activity 2

Aim

To give participants an opportunity to consider the child's perspective and to explore how the child can best be supported in sharing their views and feelings.

Method

- Distribute the case study: Involving children (page 79) as a handout.

- Divide the group into two, telling them that half of the group will take the child's perspective and half the professional's perspective.

- Divide the two groups up further into manageable working groups, e.g. four or five people.

- Those groups taking the child's perspective are to work through the following questions. (Suggest they take a few minutes individually to reflect and then discuss in their groups.)

  - You are the child. What are you thinking? Feeling? Wanting? Worried about?

  - How, if at all could someone help you feel as if you could tell them how you are feeling?

  - What do you think will happen if you are not able to tell anybody?

  - What do you think will happen if you tell somebody?

- The groups who are taking the professionals' perspective, should also reflect individually then discuss the following questions within their group:

  - What might the child's behaviour/presentation mean?

  - What might they be thinking? Feeling? Wanting? Worried about?

  - How are you most likely to find out?

- Bring the whole group back together. Ensure the 'children' have fully deroled from identifying with the child. Then ask for feedback and facilitate a group discussion, first asking the 'professionals' what they came up with and then the children. Discuss any surprises, learning points and challenges.

Activity 3

Aim

To highlight the importance of accuracy and context when sharing information given by children. Also to encourage empathy for children about whom information is shared.

Method

Undertake the Storytelling activity described in chapter 5, page 150. This team development activity can be used to explore the experience of sharing information that is meaningful with others who then pass it on. After running through the exercise, participants explore the following: How does it feel to have others talking about you? Was the meaning of what you conveyed lost in any way? Was what you described accurately and fully reported? Highlight the links and learning points in relation to children telling their stories.

Assessing need and risk for children in chronic situations

This section explores the challenges and factors to consider when undertaking assessments of children living in difficult circumstances of a chronic nature. Whilst it is not easy to make assessments and decisions of any complex situations, for example following incidents of abuse or clear harm to children, it is perhaps even more difficult to make judgements about situations that on the surface can present as more 'low-level' in harm when viewed at one point in time, but that, cumulatively, over time or when a number of factors converge can result in significant and lasting harm to children or risk to their lives. Emotional abuse and neglect are notoriously difficult to assess for this reason.

It is often the case that parental problems such as; substance misuse, mental health problems, intimate partner violence or learning difficulties are present in situations where parenting capacity is a concern. It does not automatically follow that such problems will lead to the harm of a child, particularly if appropriate support is in place and being utilised, but it does increase the likelihood (Brandon and others, 2008 and 2009, Cleaver and others 2007). This increases where more than one such difficulty coexists. Situations are further compounded when external factors such as poverty and social isolation are present.

Whilst any of the above parental problems that may affect the care of children present their own particular challenges and dynamics, both within families and between families and professionals, they often have some factors in common.

There may not be clear incidents or crises that give rise to decisive action or a clear view of the family's situation. It is more likely that deficits in the care of children and young people will be long term and chronic. Indicators are more likely to be ambiguous. The concerns and observations of professionals, taken alone may not be seen as major problems, but over time and when bringing multiple perspectives and information together, a much more worrying picture can emerge. Even when a fuller picture is seen it is difficult to 'determine the threshold for decisive action based on an accumulation of concerns' (Daniel and others 2009, Farmer and Lutman 2010).

The signs and symptoms of neglect and maltreatment are often not clearly visible to professionals, they may be open to interpretation or professionals may simply not have the awareness to pick up on them. Also, there may be uncertainty by universal and other children's services professionals about whether to refer, and confusion about thresholds, or difficulties in relationships between other professional groups and children's social care. Adult practitioners have an important role in identifying situations of potential harm to children, but they may have 'divided loyalties and different perceptions of risk of harm to children' (Davies and Ward 2011). There is still much to be done in terms of improving information sharing and joint working across the board.

Unfortunately, the above issues and increasingly high thresholds for referral and intervention mean that many children in chronic circumstances with high levels of need do not receive timely help and this is particularly an issue in cases of neglect and emotional abuse (Brandon and others 2008 and 2009, Farmer and others 2008, Ward and others 2010). Many children are left for too long or returned home prematurely to neglectful circumstances. There may be a range of reasons for this. Davies and Ward (2011) point to a lack of awareness about the impact of neglect and argue that better training on child development is needed for professionals and as part of social work training, in addition to more awareness of signs and indicators of maltreatment and of the consequences of not making timely decisions.

Even when situations of children in chronic circumstances are known about by children's social care, there still remains the difficulty of predicting what will happen in the future for the child. If left at home, will they be further harmed? There are no easy answers. Although parental cooperation and engagement is a key factor affecting decisions made following assessments (Brophy 2006, Cleaver and others 2004, Holland 2010 in Turney and others 2011), cooperation is not in itself 'an adequate predictor of parents' abilities to change sufficiently to meet the needs of the child' (Barlow 2010, Ward and others 2010 in Turney and others 2011). There will also be cases in which families are able to conceal abuse and neglect. Munro (2011) says that those involved in protecting children must be 'risk sensible'. Harm can never be totally prevented and 'decisions about risk should therefore be judged by the quality of the decision-making and not by the outcome'.

The first aim in working with families is to try and improve the child's circumstances and, provided it is in the child's interest, support them and their family to stay together. However, it is essential that support is based on a clear and full understanding and analysis of the child's needs and the family's problems. In chronic situations there is a need for targeted support that continues beyond any crisis periods due to the often long-term and 'deep-seated' nature of parental problems. Research (Fauth and others 2010) supports this, with the finding that for complex families, 'focused, long-term services appear to achieve better outcomes for children than episodic intervention'. However, Davies and Ward (2011) found that in reality cases are often closed too quickly at the first signs of improvement with little monitoring as to whether change has been sustained.

There can be understandable reluctance to remove children permanently from their families, in part added to by concerns about the care system itself. However, the evidence indicates that where there has been evidence of past abuse and neglect, maltreated children who remain looked after often fare better than those who return home (Davies and Ward 2011). They also found that around two-thirds of children who returned home subsequently became looked after again and those children who experienced repeated, failed attempts at reunification had the worst outcomes.

Issues of timing and delay in decision making are key for children. In their review of the research, Davies and Ward (2011) highlight the need for early recognition of emotional abuse and neglect in order to militate against the potential for pervasive and serious effects across all aspects of a child's development. The earlier identification and decisive action is taken, the better children's life chances. Babies are most likely to develop secure attachments to permanent carers if they are placed with them before the age of one and the first three years of a child's development are critical to the future chances. However, it is not just young children who need further attention in these circumstances. The impact of adolescent emotional abuse and neglect is widespread and Brandon and others (2008 and 2009) found the consequences in some cases were suicide or serious injury due to risk-taking behaviour.

In reality, early decisive action may not occur because there is an understandable tendency for practitioners to want to give parents the benefit of the doubt and repeated chances to achieve change, which often leads to delay or lack of decision-making

As children get older, the tendency for delay increases and the research indicates that after the age of around six, *Proactive case management tends to diminish as the chances of achieving permanency reduce, and adolescents may be the neglected both by their families and also by services* (Davies and Ward 2011).

It is not just children for whom timeframes are key, but parents also. Pregnancy and birth of a new child can be a motivator for change. However, if such change does not appear to occur during pregnancy or in the months afterwards, then it may not do so within a timescale congruent with the child's needs. It may be that some parents aren't ready to give one child what they need, but may be able to do so for a subsequent child at a later stage.

Given the impact of delay on children, it is vital to consider carefully if and when further or repeated assessments are really necessary to avoid the 'start again syndrome' described by Brandon and others (2008 and 2009). This involves considering if there has already been sufficient time for change to occur and what is the purpose of further assessment? Hart and Powell (2007) noted that in the case of parents with problem drug use, residential assessments were sometimes regarded as a 'safe place to fail' and went ahead, adding further delay, when there was little indication or expectation of them being successful.

So what supports effective assessments and decision-making in such circumstances? The foundation for building a good assessment lies in forming constructive relationships with parents wherever possible. Barlow and Scott (2010) in Munro (2011) reported on the importance of: 'a dependable professional relationship for parents and children, in particular with those families who conceal or minimise the difficulties'.

Striking the right balance and setting the tone when working directly with parents and children requires sensitivity, self-awareness, respect and good professional judgement. In order to support parents to better meet their children's needs; and in order to understand the parents, the way they think, their motivation, their previous experiences and their hopes for the future, it is important to be able to engage constructively with them and try to gain their trust and to convey genuine concern and interest in them. However, it is also necessary to be challenging, maintain a healthy scepticism and be authoritative where necessary, honest and clear. Failing to strike the right balance can result in an overconcentration on parents and being diverted from the needs of the child, or, conversely, entering into an 'adversarial relationship with the parents' at the cost of successful engagement (Munro 2011).

In a submission to the Munro review, the Family Rights Group identified some obstacles to engagement with families, including a lack of clarity in the way professionals' concerns were explained to them. They also stressed that the processes and formal meetings can be overwhelming for families and the strong emotions the process evokes can prevent them from hearing what is being said by the local authority. 'They are not supported to take responsibility. Instead decisions and actions are done "to" rather than "with" them, which encourages a sense of dependency and resentment' (Munro 2011).

There is a need for practitioners to demonstrate a recognition of the fear and confusion parents can experience in these situations in order to attempt to overcome obstacles to trust and openness (some of these issues are discussed further in the Signs of safety model in this chapter).

The changes required for children in chronic situations usually require significant shifts in parental attitude and behaviour. This will entail overcoming habits of thought and action. In exploring with service users if such change is possible and likely, it is important to understand their perspective on this and their previous experiences of trying to change. The Cycle of change model, often applied by those working in substance misuse services, sets out a process by which people move through the stages of change listed below.

1. **Pre-contemplation** The person sees no reason to change their behavior, whatever the advice offered.

2. **Contemplation** The person considers making a change at some point in the future, but is still unsure about making a firm commitment to it.

3. **Preparation** A decision to change is taken, the person takes some personal responsibility for the desired changes and starts planning to take action.

4. **Action** The person actively pursues the desired change. Observable effort is made to break with old habits or to develop a new, more positive, one.

5. **Maintenance** The desired change has been achieved, and lasted for some time. The main task at this stage is to prevent oneself from slipping back into old habits (relapse prevention).

(Adapted from Prochaska and others 1994)

When trying to change entrenched behaviours, people may go through stages 1 to 4 numerous times, each time relapsing, before achieving maintenance of the change, if at all. It can be helpful in assessing the progress of change to understand the above process (and to support parents to understand it) in order to provide support that is timely, and targeted at where parents are at in relation to the cycle. This understanding may also assist in decisions about likelihood of change at a given time. It can also be useful in helping to establish patterns that occur, for example leading to mental health relapse, parental conflict or drug use, in order to find ways of identifying early when relapse is likely to occur and help parents plan strategies to make maintenance of the change more likely.

In addition to understanding and assessing the potential for change, it is also important to assess parental motivation. Once again, the way parents are approached can be key to this. Challenging and confronting people or 'trying to make them see or admit' to the extent of their problems may be necessary, but it is important to understand that such an approach can increase the likelihood of people feeling defensive, feeling the need to hide things or withdrawing from professionals altogether. Statutory children and families services often use such approaches when there are child protection concerns. Practitioners in such services, and in fact all practitioners trying to engage with people who they feel are 'resistant', should consider critically the extent to which their practices are unintentionally reinforcing such denial. Miller and Rollnick (2002) argue that good empathic listening, which is at the heart of their Motivational Interviewing (MI) approach, is far more productive.

The four general principles of the MI approach are as follows.

1. **Express empathy** Is fundamental to effectiveness. 'Acceptance' of people 'as they are' seems to free people up to change. Ambivalence is a normal part of human experience.

2. **Develop discrepancy** as MI is intentionally directive (unlike person-centred counselling). The goal is to amplify the discrepancy between the person's behaviour and their goals or values.

3. **Roll with resistance** otherwise, if the counsellor advocates change and the client argues against it, it is counter-productive and may even push the client further in the opposite direction. New perspectives are invited (from the client by turning questions or problems back on the person) and not imposed.

4. **Support self-efficacy** this refers to a person's belief in his or her ability to succeed with something and is an important part of motivation. A counsellor's belief in a client's ability to change can create a self-fulfilling prophecy.

Forrester (2004) argues that social workers (and others) would benefit from attempting to apply the principles of an MI approach in their work. Through research, Forrester found that for some practitioners, basic training in the approach improved listening skills, resulted in a less confrontational style, a reduced tendency to impose a social work agenda and, as a result, an increased ability to engage constructively with service users (Forrester 2004, Forrester and Harwin 2008). Whilst this approach was being explored with substance misusing parents specifically, other research has shown it to have wider applications, so the skills and principles could apply more broadly to chronic situations where parental problems are a factor.

Where professionals are engaged in doing all they can to understand, motivate and engage with parents, it is absolutely crucial that this does not cause them to lose sight of the child's immediate well-being. Children of course should have their views explored effectively (this issue is discussed more fully in chapter 2). This involves continuously seeking to understand; what is their day-to-day experience? What are their needs? What will be the impact on them if these are not met and if the concerns about them remain?

Practitioners also need to guard against becoming desensitised to low standards of parenting and care, as neglect can become 'normalised', not just in the mind of family members, but to those around them including professionals when they are exposed to particular families over long periods of time. Appointing a co-worker to visit occasionally and support the allocated worker in considering thresholds of intervention might help (Farmer and Lutman 2009) with this as will high quality supervision.

In assessing parental capacity, it is essential that practitioners have an understanding of what is required of parents and of their ability to change (Jones, 2009 in Turney and others 2011). This extends to all significant adults on whom the child depends. It is important to stress this, given that father's are often not sufficiently included within assessments. This will involve assessing all carers in respect of: their commitment to maintaining the family unit and/or their commitment to their relationship with the child; their capacity to be available/intervene on the child's behalf if and when necessary; any history of conflict and abuse between partners and their capacity to work together as parents (Gopfert and others 2004).

Family functioning and family history are key to an assessment of need and risk. Research has shown that 'the best predictors of multi-type maltreatment are poor family cohesion (family members being disconnected from one another), low family adaptability (rigid roles and inflexibility in relationships and communication) and the poor quality of the adult relationship' (Higgins and McCabe, 2000).

The importance of creating a comprehensive chronology to ascertain the child's history, the parent's history, past events within the family, the nature of previous interventions and their outcome and to see patterns over time cannot be stressed enough (Brandon and others 2008 and 2009, Farmer and Lutman 2009). This will help in considering the parents potential for change. It is also helpful to have an annual summary of long-term cases available in the file (Turney and others 2011).

As has been stressed throughout this toolkit, using a range of methods and sources for the assessment is crucial. It is important to try and avoid an overreliance on parents' verbal articulacy in demonstrating their cooperation and insight (Holland 2004, Turney and others 2011). A variety of approaches to gathering information can be used. Validated tools such as the Strengths and Difficulties Questionnaire or the Home Inventory (Department of Health and others 2000) can be helpful in obtaining baseline information. Other information will be gained through observation, a consideration of family history and any recent changes.

It may be necessary to organise for specialist assessments to be undertaken, for example child mental health assessment, paediatric assessment, psychological assessments of adults or children, educational or adult offending assessments. Some helpful models and checklists for assessing specific circumstances have also been created in relation to specific circumstances such as mental health, for example, Gopfert, Webster and Nelki (2004) Dimensions of parenting formulation, or in relation to alcohol misusing parents, tools such as the Alcohol Use Questionnaire (Department of Health and others 2000).

Where adult services are involved in supporting a parent with their problems, for example specialist substance misuse workers, it is helpful for children's practitioners to work alongside them to increase their understanding of the adult's problems and progress. Even where specialist services are not involved or required, there is undoubtedly value in gaining a range of professional perspectives. In Turney and others (2011), the importance of coordinated multiagency assessment is highlighted in entrenched situations where families have multiple difficulties. They found that where such assessments took place, children were more likely to be returned home safely.

Finally, it is important given how emotionally and mentally challenging assessment and decision-making in such circumstances can be, that high-quality supervision, support and reflection time is available to practitioners, supporting them in avoiding delays in decision-making whilst doing all they can to improve children's circumstances within their families. The challenge is in knowing where to 'draw the line'.

The following tool is intended as a prompt to aid thinking and focus practitioner's minds on the nature and extent of harm that children are experiencing, the reasons for this and considerations of timing in decision-making.

Practice tool 8: Considering impact and harm in chronic situations

1. Does this appear to be long-term chronic neglect or an acute response to a family's current circumstance?
Details:
2. What evidence is there of Persistence? Have neglect/concerns been present over a significant period of time?
Details:
3. Have efforts to intervene, to minimise or prevent the neglect/concerns been made? If so what? Have these efforts had any significant impact in the past?
Details:
4. What aspects of the child's care are of concern? In which areas are they neglected or are their needs not consistently met?
❏ child's basic physical needs
Details:
❏ child's emotional and attachment needs
Details:
❏ child's cognitive development
Details:
❏ child's medical needs
Details:
❏ child's needs for safety and security
Details:
❏ exclusion from home or abandonment
Details:
❏ failing to protect a child from physical and emotional harm or danger
Details:
❏ unresponsiveness to a child's basic emotional needs
Details:
❏ is it **global** – are all or most areas of a child's development impacted upon?
Details:

5. What is the actual or potential harm to the child/young person? Specify evidence of actual harm and reasons for concerns about potential harm.
❏ short-term (including impact on day to day life)
Details:
❏ medium-term
Details:
❏ long-term (making reference to research findings)
Details:
6. What is driving the failure to provide care by carer?
❏ poverty
Details:
❏ lack of skills, knowledge or insight into child's needs
Details:
❏ lack of skills, knowledge or insight into child's needs plus social isolation
Details:
❏ parenting capacity (Which aspects of parenting capacity are of concern? How is this demonstrated and/or why are you concerned?)
Details: <ul><li>basic care</li><li>ensuring safety</li><li>emotional warmth</li><li>stimulation</li><li>guidance and boundaries</li><li>stability</li></ul>
❏ domestic violence/abuse
Details:
❏ learning disability
Details:
❏ substance misuse
Details:
❏ mental health issues
Details:
❏ parental separation, divorce or conflict
Details:
❏ lack of a relationship of care and/or lack of parental motivation
Details:
7. Does this appear to be an act of omission or commission and how is this affecting your thinking?
Details:

8. Do you have information available which suggest an intergenerational pattern of neglect or abuse in this family?

Details:

9. What other kinds of abuse is the neglect driving or enabling? This may include concerns about what might happen. Be clear if abuse is actual or potential.

 ❏ sexual abuse

Details:

 ❏ physical abuse

Details:

 ❏ emotional abuse

Details:

10. What key strengths/protective factors have been identified and to what extent are these protecting the child from harm?

Details:

11. Using your professional judgement. On a scale of 0–10 rate how severe you believe the neglect/harm to be. (Where 0 is no neglect/harm, 5 is a likelihood of significant harm if the situation continues and 10 is so severe that the threshold for significant harm has been met or exceeded.) Provide evidence for your reasoning below.

0 1 2 3 4 5 6 7 8 9 10
evidence...

12. Rate on a scale of 0–10 the need for statutory intervention. (0 means that no action would be taken by your agency, 5 means intervention is required to address the deficits in care and/or to monitor and protect the child, and 10 means that the child needs to be removed to a place of safety immediately, or that statutory proceedings need to be instigated e.g. Sec 47 or PLO.) Please give your reasoning below.

0 1 2 3 4 5 6 7 8 9 10
reasoning...

13. Rate on a scale of 0–10 the likelihood of the parent/carer being able to respond to intervention and make and sustain sufficient change to provide a safe and secure environment for the child/children in the future. Give your reasoning below.

0 1 2 3 4 5 6 7 8 9 10
reasoning...

14. How do considerations of timing affect what needs to happen? For example within what timescale does significant change need to occur for the child? Is this achievable?

Details:

Use your analysis of the responses you have given to the questions above to help in case discussions, planning and decision-making. There is no scoring sheet for this questionnaire, but completion will help in developing an informed view of the complexity of the neglect and the likely prospect for change.

This tool has been adapted from a questionnaire developed by Jane Wiffin 2009

Case study: Children in chronic situations

Tiffany Carter	1 year and 10 months	Subject
Keely Carter	5 years	Subject
Rowan Miller	8 years	Subject
Paula Miller	15 years	Sister of Rowan, lives with maternal grandmother
Stephanie Carter	32 years	Mother
Grant Carter	27 years	Father of Tiffany and Keely
Keith Miller	36 years	Father of Rowan and Paula

You are the social worker and have been allocated this case with the suggestion by your supervisor that you review the case notes and pull together a chronology because the family has been known to the team for years now with intermittent contact and little apparent improvement in parenting.

Based on your review of the file you establish the following

When Paula was seven, her school were concerned about her and made a referral. They described her as looking constantly tired, pale and 'grey' with dark circles under her eyes and frequent cold sores. She had also been overheard telling another child that the police had been to her house because her mum and dad were arguing and her dad had made a hole in the door. The school had made two appointments with Stephanie and Keith to discuss their concerns, but they had not attended either. The family was then visited by a duty worker. Stephanie was seven months pregnant and said she had been exhausted and forgetful, which is why she had forgotten the school appointments and that Paula's dad, Keith had left the home two months ago and they were now separated. Her washing machine had broken and she was given financial support to purchase another.

There was some further involvement when Paula was nine. The school reported that she was behind her peers in terms of progress with her learning and found it difficult to make friends, tending to gravitate towards adults instead. Her hair often looked unwashed and tangled for days. Her mum seemed to have had a couple of partners since the previous referral and sometimes different people arrived to collect Paula from school without the school having been notified, including Paula's dad, Keith, on occasion. At one point Stephanie had told them she didn't want Keith to collect Paula, but now she didn't seem to mind.

An assessment was carried out. Stephanie said she had recently split up from a boyfriend, Gary she had been with for four months. She said that the children still had occasional contact with Paula and Rowan's father, Keith, 'when he felt like it'. She said he had 'calmed down' these days. She seemed willing to accept help, saying Paula always made such a fuss when she tried to wash her hair and that she had started 'putting it off'. She did not know why Paula was behind at school, but seemed to view it as inevitable saying that she was the same when she was at school and Paula was probably 'a bit thick, like me'.

When checks were carried out, the health visitor said they had not seen a great deal of Rowan (then nearly two) at clinic, but his weight though slightly below average was not unhealthy. He was not vocalising much, but Stephanie reported that he was having tantrums. She agreed to attend a course of behaviour management classes with Rowan. She had attended two out of three at the time of the last case entry. It is not known if she attended the rest and there appeared to be no further intervention at this stage.

Nearly three years later, when Rowan was five, his school made a referral. He had recently started school and was not settling in very well. He was described as looking quite unkempt and grubby at times and sometimes having 'a bit of a smell'. His concentration was poor and his speech and language was quite delayed compared to his peers.

An assessment was carried out. Stephanie had had another baby, Keely, whose father, Grant Carter was now living with the family.

Paula (now 12 years old) had recently gone to live with her grandmother. Stephanie said it was because Paula liked it there because she got more attention (which Stephanie found difficult to give as much of since the birth of Keely).

The health visitor reported that Keely's weight was just within normal limits, although below-average, but there had been a drop in weight in the last couple of months which seemed unusual. When the health visitor went to the family home at the request of the social worker she reported that the home conditions were 'poor'. Also she had expressed her concern to the family that Keely seemed to be left strapped into her high chair in front of the TV when she visited and it did not seem to be a meal time. She had no food in front of her and no toys either.

The social work assessment at the time also indicated concerns about home conditions: dirty cot bedding; a 'musty smell'; half finished DIY projects with tools lying around in the hallway (still there two weeks after the social worker originally pointed these out); an overflowing bin in the kitchen; and sticky looking worktops in the kitchen. Two announced home visits were frustrated by the parents not being in or not answering the door and a child protection conference was convened. Rowan and Keely were made subjects of a child protection plan. At the review conference three months later, this ceased as the home conditions had improved significantly as had Rowan's physical presentation at school. While there were still some concerns about the extent to which Stephanie understood why social services had been so worried, Grant appeared to grasp this and was instrumental in making the changes, frequently contacting social workers himself to tell them what he had done. It was agreed that the case would be monitored, but from case records it seemed that social work involvement had fizzled out after this.

Having now updated network checks and undertaken a visit to the family (although Grant was not present at the time), you have established the following

The school continues to have concerns about Rowan. His teacher suspects he undertakes some of the care of his younger siblings as he has referred to having to get Keely up for school and has twice sustained injuries, once a small cut from a knife he said he was using to make dinner for him and Keely and on another occasion, an iron burn on the side of his hand.

Keely's teacher has also logged some concerns in recent months. She had been unsure if these met the threshold for referral, so was monitoring. When playing in the home corner Keely is often quite aggressive when mimicking a parent: pointing in other children's faces, threatening to hit them and saying 'shut up or you won't have any tea' and 'I told you to stay in your room'. Keely has also had head lice a few times, which they suspect is not treated properly. Grant became annoyed when this was raised with him, saying she was getting it from her classmates, but the teacher says it is only Keely in her class who keeps getting it. Rowan has had head lice recently too. The teacher also noted that Keely is clingy with school staff and her behaviour with other children is erratic and often aggressive causing others to find her difficult to get on with.

Tiffany is slightly underweight and the health visitor has not seen much of her. On the last three occasions when she was weighed she had nappy rash. You have observed her to be not very responsive to your presence when visiting. On the last two occasions she was just in her nappy, although it was not warm inside the house and you suggested she might need more clothes on.

Stephanie has told you she had an 'interfering' social worker when she was a teenager and she used to be scared of social workers, but she thinks 'you're alright really'.

You have been in touch with Paula's school, but not yet met her. The school reported that she is often in trouble, and recently had a fight with another girl who alleged that she had stolen from her. The school say she has been sent to school on occasions when she seemed too unwell to be there. They find the grandmother unresponsive, for example to phone calls home when Paula has been unwell. Also, the grandmother often refers them to Stephanie, telling them to 'leave her out of it', leading the school to wonder who is taking responsibility for Paula. They have also heard Paula refer to her 'mum's boyfriend', (presumably, Grant) as 'an alcy' (alcoholic) and when teachers have told Paula that her parents/grandmother will be notified when she has been in trouble, she said, 'say what you want. They don't give a toss.'

You have contacted the local authority where Stephanie used to live to find out more about social work involvement in her childhood and are awaiting feedback. You don't know much yet about the backgrounds of Grant Carter or Keith Miller.

Considering impact and harm in chronic situations

(The answers below are in relation to all the children – although the form could be used for just one child. These are only an example of the sort of answers that could be given.)

1. Does this appear to be long-term chronic neglect or an acute response to a family's current circumstance?
Details: *Chronic neglect*
2. What evidence is there of persistence? Have neglect/concerns been present over a significant period of time?
Details: *Yes. The same kind of problems seem to have occurred over a number of years, affecting all children in the family. This seems to date back at least eight years to when Paula was aged seven.*
3. Have efforts to intervene, to minimise or prevent the neglect/concerns been made? If so what? Have these efforts had any significant impact in the past?
Details: *Some practical support, some exploration of the problems with the parents, behaviour management sessions, advice from health visitors and social workers, a previous child protection plan. The impact of these efforts seems to have only temporarily made an impact, although the child protection plan made a significant impact, but this wasn't lasting.*
4. What aspects of the child's care are of concern? In which areas are they neglected or are their needs not consistently met?
❏ child's basic physical needs
Details: *Yes, there have been concerns about this in the past for Paula and in the past and currently for Rowan, Keely and Tiffany.*
❏ child's emotional and attachment needs
Details: *Yes, there are concerns about all four children in terms of their emotional well-being and attachment behaviour.*
❏ child's cognitive development
Details: *Still to be ascertained re: Paula. Further checks and questions to be asked about this for all children. Rowan was showing language delay at age 5 – what about now?*
❏ child's medical needs
Details: *Possibly untreated nappy rash of Tiffany. Check out if Rowan's cut and iron burn injuries were treated appropriately by parents. Indications of Paula being sent to school when unwell.*
❏ child's needs for safety and security
Details: *There are indicators of concern in this area; Rowan's injuries; previous concerns about home conditions, various people collecting from school, Paula's unclear guardianship, previous domestic violence? Alcohol misuse?*
❏ exclusion from home or abandonment
Details: *Uncertain circumstances regarding Paula's care.*

❏ failing to protect a child from physical and emotional harm or danger

Details: *Possibly. Rowan's previous injuries, previous domestic violence? Likely lack of supervision in context of wider neglect.*

❏ unresponsiveness to a child's basic emotional needs

Details: *Likely. See concerns regarding Paula's possible rejection from family and current problems, Rowan's presentation and Keeley's (relationships with peers, cleanliness, behaviour in home corner); also Tiffany's unresponsiveness.*

❏ is it **global** – are all or most areas of a child's development impacted upon?

Details: *Yes*

5. What is the actual or potential harm to the child/young person? Specify evidence of actual harm and reasons for concerns about potential harm.

❏ short-term (including impact on day to day life)

Details: *Adverse impact on physical well-being and development currently (for the three younger children particularly, and need to look into nature of Paula's ill health referred to by school). Also, concerns for all children about relationships with peers, ability to learn, emotional well-being (not known how Paula is, that needs to be established), safety.*

❏ medium-term

Details: *All unlikely to achieve optimum health, poor educational progress, adverse impact on emotional well-being and ability to form attachments and social relationships. Possible 'failure to thrive' for Tiffany. Risks through physical neglect or emotional problems or lack of supervision could lead to incidents of significant harm and/or accumulated psychological damage.*

❏ Long-term (making reference to research findings)

Details: *Potential for long-term health problems, lack of opportunities, choice and employment in the future. As above, cumulative effects on emotional and psychological well-being. Impact on ability to form relationships. Likelihood of affecting own parenting in the future – 'cycles of deprivation'.*

6. What is driving the failure to provide care by carer?

❏ poverty

Details: *Not known. Maybe an issue, but not the main issue.*

❏ lack of skills, knowledge or insight into child's needs

Details: *Possibly. Needs further exploration.*

❏ lack of skills, knowledge or insight into child's needs plus social isolation

Details: *As above.*

❏ parenting capacity (Which aspects of parenting capacity are of concern? How is this demonstrated and/or why are you concerned?)

Details:

- basic care – *Yes, tiredness, getting own meals? Recurrent nappy rash and head lice, unkempt etc.*
- ensuring safety – *Rowan's previous injuries, lack of supervision?, home conditions, protection from other adults? Need to assess impact of alcohol further.*
- emotional warmth – *See concerns regarding children's relationships, Paula's comments, Keely's behaviour in the 'home corner' and Tiffany's unresponsiveness.*
- stimulation – *Seems to be lacking. See current presentation of Tiffany and previous observations of Keely as a baby.*
- guidance and boundaries – *Behavioural concerns re Rowan previously and Keely currently, Paula stealing and fighting.*
- stability – *Previously, apparent changes in partners and various people picking up from school, Paula's unclear situation.*

❏ domestic violence/abuse

Details: *Query regarding past incidents of police being called when Keith lived in the home. What's his current relationship/contact?*

❏ learning disability

Details: *Possibly (see Stephanie's reference to herself as 'thick') – is there a level of learning difficulty? Stephanie's apparent lack of understanding of concerns in the past.*

❏ substance misuse

Details: *Assessment needed regarding alcohol use of Grant and its impact.*

❏ mental health issues

Details: *Not known to be impacting.*

❏ parental separation, divorce or conflict

Details: *Lots of changes/various relationships. Need to know more about quality and dynamics of current relationship between Stephanie and Grant.*

❏ lack of a relationship of care and/or lack of parental motivation

Details: *The prolonged nature of the problems, the attitudes recently when asked about head lice and the fact that the problems were addressed in the context of a child protection plan, but resumed shortly afterwards raise serious concerns about motivation and relationship of care. Also, see Paula's recent comments.*

7. Does this appear to be an act of omission or commission and how is this affecting your thinking?

Details: *Certainly omission over the years, but possibly commission too (see Keeley's behaviour in home corner, for example).*

8. Do you have information available which suggest an intergenerational pattern of neglect or abuse in this family?

Details: *Some social work involvement in Stephanie's past. Needs further exploration in respect of this and the histories in both fathers' families, and grandparents.*

9. What other kinds of abuse is the neglect driving or enabling? This may include concerns about what might happen. Be clear if abuse is actual or potential.

❏ sexual abuse

Details: *Not known of, but increased vulnerability of children due to neglect, clinginess to adults and possible lack of supervision/emotional care to Paula.*

❏ physical abuse

Details: *Not known of, but need to have open mind regarding previous injuries to Rowan and Keeley's ' 'home corner' behaviour.*

❏ emotional abuse

Details: *This may already be happening. Certainly a lack of emotional care seems to be present and possibly 'low warmth/high criticism' environment (for example, see Keeley's behaviour).*

10. **What key strengths/protective factors have been identified and to what extent are these protecting the child from harm?**

Details: *Unclear to what extent grandmother is a protective factor and her attitude when contacted by school raises concerns. Grant previously showed himself able to make changes, but didn't sustain these, which raises concerns about his motivation.*

11. **Using your professional judgement.** On a scale of 0–10 rate how severe you believe the neglect/harm to be. (Where 0 is no neglect/harm, 5 is a likelihood of significant harm if the situation continues and 10 is so severe that the threshold for significant harm has been met or exceeded). Provide evidence for your reasoning below.

0 1 2 3 4 5 6 7 <u>8</u> <u>9</u> <u>10</u>
Evidence: *Need to look at each child individually, but when taken as a whole, the situation is of serious concern. Further assessment is necessary of specific information gaps, but enough is known to indicate likely current harm and future significant harm.*

12. **Rate on a scale of 0–10 the need for statutory intervention.** (0 means that no action would be taken by your agency, 5 means intervention is required to address the deficits in care and/or to monitor and protect the child, and 10 means that the child needs to be removed to a place of safety immediately, or that statutory proceedings need to be instigated e.g. Sec 47 or PLO.) Please give your reasoning below.

0 1 2 3 4 5 6 7 <u>8</u> <u>9</u> <u>10</u>
Reasoning: *As above, robust, time-limited and targeted intervention based on a clear understanding of the problems and areas that need to change is required, with consideration to be given to proceedings.*

13. **Rate on a scale of 0–10 the likelihood of the parent/carer being able to respond to intervention and make and sustain sufficient change to provide a safe and secure environment for the child / children in the future.** Give your reasoning below.

0 1 2 <u>3</u> <u>4</u> <u>5</u> 6 7 8 9 10
Reasoning: *Some engagement, willingness to respond to concerns raised. Did make changes in past, but did not sustain these and have not made significant changes over a long period of time.*

14. **How do considerations of timing affect what needs to happen?** For example within what timescale does significant change need to occur for the child? Is this achievable?
Details: *Is not in the children's interest for this situation to continue and the risks are high that this will affect their future development and limit their potential. For this reason if further efforts are to be made, e.g. in the context of another child protection plan, this needs to be robustly monitored and time-limited with decisions about the long-term made sooner rather than later. In terms of Tiffany's physical and cognitive development any delay may be significantly detrimental.*

Use your analysis of the responses you have given to the questions above to help in case discussions, planning and decision-making. There is no scoring sheet for this questionnaire but completion will help in developing an informed view of the complexity of the neglect and the likely prospect for change.

This tool has been adapted from a questionnaire developed by Jane Wiffin 2009.

Practice development session 8: Assessing need and risk for children in chronic situations

Aim

To consider the particular challenges that arise in assessments and decision-making for children in chronic situations. To explore what aids workers in promoting change and making timely decisions.

Method

- Invite discussion regarding the particular challenges of working with children in chronic situations of neglect and abuse. Ask participants how often such situations are accompanied by parental problems in their experience, such as domestic violence, substance misuse, mental health problems. What do they find difficult to influence/decide upon? What helps them in these circumstances?

- Give a brief presentation about conducting assessments with children in chronic situations, using slides from presentation 8. Slides 78–83. Download from www.ncb.org.uk/support/resources

- Give out the practice tool 'Considering impact and harm in chronic situations'. Explain to participants that the tool can be used as a prompt to thinking. It does not require detailed answers as the information should be held within assessments and elsewhere, but it might focus their thinking and help them to make more confident judgements about the likelihood or presence of harm.

- Give out copies of case study: Children in chronic situations (page 93). Depending on time, participants, working in pairs or groups are instructed to fill out the questionnaire with one child from the family in mind, or with regard to all the children (as in the example on page 96). Either way, they will draw on all the known background information in their thinking.

Or

- Participants can use the tool in relation to a real case, working individually or in pairs if the case is co-worked. If this is a team session, one member could present a case and they could discuss the questions as a group.

- Invite feedback. Were some questions particularly difficult to answer? Was it easy or difficult to reach agreement if working in pairs or groups? Were any answers unexpected or surprising? Did the tool elicit ideas and thoughts that may have otherwise been missed? Did it clarify areas about which more information was needed? How might this tool be applied usefully in practice?

4. Making, recording and reviewing decisions

Decision-making

In her book *Effective Child Protection* (2002) Eileen Munro explores approaches to decision-making in social work over the last hundred years, commenting that social work has been hampered in building a reliable and consistent evidence base as a result of shifting fashions. Munro explores the potential role of decision theory in social work with children and families.

She states that decision theory rationally portrays people as thoughtful decision-makers, considering alternative actions, deliberating about their consequences; and choosing an option that seems most likely to satisfy goals.

Munro identifies, however, that studies that show how people *actually* reason are striking in the extent to which they show the reluctance of people to make decisions.

In child protection work reluctance to make decisions shows up in a tendency to procrastinate, so that decisions are made in reaction to a crisis rather than a long-term plan. Children in care are particularly vulnerable to failure in active decision-making – and this often results in drift, poor planning and a lack of decisions about contact. According to Munro the same type of drift also shows up in research on child protection, where there is a lack of proactive planning and a tendency to react to crises as they occur. The introduction of timescales is one attempt that has been made towards addressing this problem, which has gone some way towards standardising the practice in the Looked After Children (LAC) system and in assessment.

However, decision-making is a hard task and is both intellectually and emotionally challenging. It can also be hard because decisions often offer imperfect solutions and this can be demoralising. Sharing power is also complex – decisions require a juggling act to give due weight to a range of opinions.

Different schools of thought

Munro highlights two schools of thought that are particularly relevant to thinking about decision-making in social work.

- Decision theorists draw on probability theory and logic to prescribe a model for making decisions.

- Naturalists aim to describe how people actually make decisions.

She suggests that we can draw useful lessons from both schools. While interviewing families, a practitioner will continuously be making many intuitive micro decisions; whereas a decision about whether or not to remove a child from their family will require considerable deliberation and need to be justifiable to the family and legal systems.

Formal decision theory offers a framework for organising reasoning and ensuring that details are not overlooked. Decision theory can help in situations where professionals are feeling confused or overwhelmed by all the factors. Decision theory and more specifically decision trees, which is a formal tool emerging from decision theory, break decisions down into component parts. They are useful in major decision-making when the importance of the subject, for example the well-being of the child, infers significant responsibility on the decider to make the best possible decision. Whilst certainty about the efficacy of a particular decision might be nigh on impossible to reach, it is important to be able to be open and clear and able to demonstrate how decisions were reached.

Decision trees set out a framework for considering possible options; considering the consequences and how probable they are; judging how good or bad those outcomes would be; and picking the option that you believe will have the most beneficial consequence. The framework uses a methodology to decide the utility value of decisions made.

Decision trees are an effective way of organising reasoning and analysing the problem. A clear identification of a sequence of events, and the links between them, in itself makes problematic decisions much easier to understand and manage. By making estimates of the probability (likelihood) and desirability of consequences explicit in terms of numbers, it is possible to work out which option has the highest value and show the grounds for the final choice.

Framework for decision trees

1. What decision is to be made?

2. What options are there?

3. What information is needed to help make the choice?

4. What are the likely/possible consequences of each option?

5. How probable is each consequence?

6. What are the pros and cons (desirability) of each consequence?

7. The final decision

The strength of the decision tree is that it makes you think widely. This can also be a disadvantage in that it can generate too much information. Judgement is needed to decide how much effort to put into the decision and therefore how much information to generate. Experience can help the practitioner to reduce the detail to which they need to apply the framework. Hammond (in Munro 2002) suggests applying one's energies to the stages of the decision framework that are most problematic. Quite often when one scans through the whole process it is possible to identify which points can be decided on easily and which ones are the most crucial or difficult for that particular decision.

It is important not to exaggerate the objectivity of decision theory. Although it uses mathematics it is crucial that the practitioner uses their own judgement in giving utility values to the outcomes and assessing their probability, but using the tree does help to push the decision along the analytic–intuitive continuum towards becoming more analytic. It helps break a complicated decision down into smaller and simpler parts. It assists, but does not replace, the human decision-maker.

The decision framework need not be followed in detail in every situation. Professionals can use it to sketch an overview of the decision they are facing and then concentrate on the problematical elements. It encourages people to make their intuitive reasoning explicit and then think it through more thoroughly. It does not remove subjectivity from the process and two rational people will not necessarily reach the same conclusions. It does help to identify where and why they would disagree however, and also provides a clear and defensible account of how a decision was reached, something which may be especially helpful in the current climate.

Practice tool 9: Decision tree

Instructions for completing a decision tree.

Read these instructions alongside the decision tree illustration (page 104).

1. What is the decision to be made? Enter data into square on left of tree.

2. What are the possible choices (options)? Enter up to four different options. Write these along the radiating lines coming out of the square.

3. What are the possible consequences of the different options? Create the same number of consequences for each option (3 or 4) and write them along the lines radiating from the circles.

4. Try and give a score to the probability (likelihood) of each consequence occurring. Score somewhere between 0 per cent and 100 per cent (0 per cent = certainly not and 100 per cent = certainly will). The total score across the consequences for one option should equal 100 per cent. You will be likely to use research evidence, practice experience, and discussion and debate to help you decide on this. Place the score in the triangle.

5. Try and decide on the desirability of each consequence occurring. Ascribe a score from 0–10 (0 = least desirable, 10 = totally desirable). These do not need to total up to 10. You have to use your judgement to decide on the desirability: by weighing up the impact on the child, their family, the wider society, cost to agency, etc. Place this score in the last box on the right.

6. Multiply each probability score by each desirability score, and then add these together for each option. This gives you a total score for each option. Place this score in the square inside the tree. The option with the highest overall score should be the best option for you to choose as it combines realistic likelihood of success with best desirability.

Decision tree

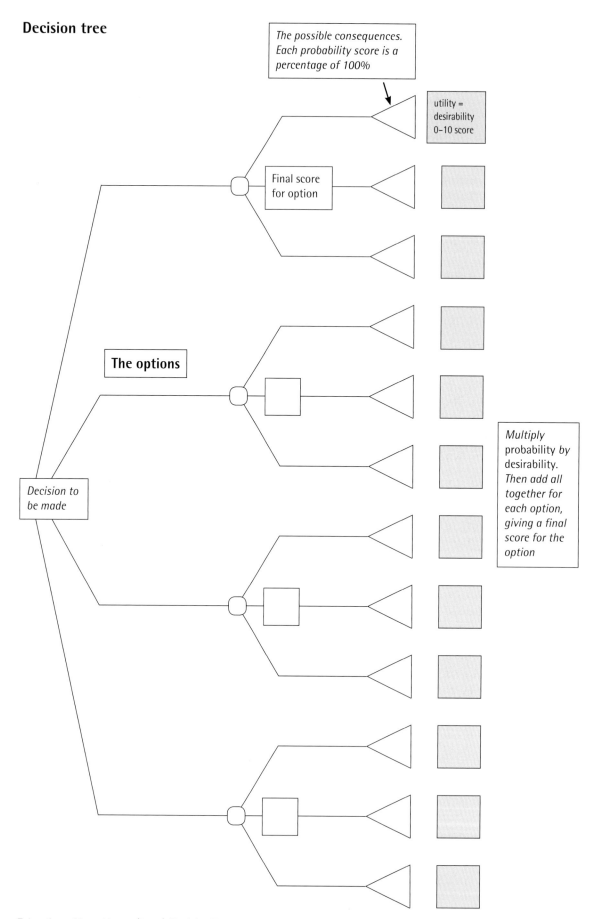

Taken from Eileen Munro (2002) 'Decision Tree', *Effective Child Protection*. Sage Publications.

Case study: Decision tree

Name	Gender	Ethnicity	Age	Relationship
Sheila White [nee Philips]	female	White British	45	mother of Paul
Gerald White	male	White British	50	father of Paul
Paul White	male	White British	8	subject (child)
Nancy Philips	female	White British	70	maternal grandmother to Paul

Paul White is the only child of Gerald and Sheila White. Gerald and Sheila married when Gerald was 40 and Sheila 35. Gerald had been in the Royal Marines, Sheila in the WRAF. They met while on active service and left the services and married in 1996. Both Gerald and Sheila had problems with excessive alcohol consumption whilst in the forces. Gerald had been referred for treatment on two separate occasions prior to his discharge and he narrowly avoided dishonourable discharge.

Sheila had been a very heavy drinker leading to some health problems but it was not until they set up their own home and Sheila became pregnant with Paul that her difficulties came to the attention of health services. Paul was born one month prematurely and was underweight. He was diagnosed as having mild foetal alcohol syndrome, which left him with some mild facial abnormalities and poor muscle tone.

Physically, Paul has few problems now, apart from poor coordination, but his emotional and behavioural development has continued to cause concern. A special needs assessment was triggered by the nursery that Paul attended from the age of three, because of his flat, unresponsive and withdrawn manner and because he seemed to be exhibiting some developmental delay. Although he has attended mainstream school since he was five, he now has a special needs statement and receives some extra support in school.

The White family have been known to Social Services since Paul's birth.

An assessment was undertaken at the time of his birth (not using the assessment framework) but, as Sheila appeared to be seeking help and attended a support programme through the local alcohol service, no other services were offered. The school Paul attends has expressed concern to Social Services about the care given to Paul by his parents at times when their drinking was getting out of control on two occasions in the past two years. They felt that he was possibly getting himself up and ready for school and walking to school in the morning, often arriving seeming very tired and hungry. Several reports by neighbours about fighting and neglect have also been received around these times.

An initial assessment was undertaken on the first occasion; but Paul went to stay with his maternal grandmother round the corner for a few weeks, until Sheila got some help and managed to get her drinking under control, and the case was closed. Sheila always seemed to want to work with the school and other agencies to address her son's needs but usually after a reasonable start, matters would deteriorate again.

Paul spoke at the time of wanting to stay with his mummy and daddy but he also told his teacher that daddy was poorly and needed to sleep on the sofa. Two months ago, the school made a referral in partnership with Paul's maternal grandmother, Nancy. The situation in the family home had deteriorated significantly.

Gerald had been drinking extremely heavily for months and was experiencing severe health problems. He had been admitted to hospital at the weekend suffering from suspected liver failure. He had accepted that he needed help and was saying currently that he was willing to cooperate with health services.

Sheila had also been drinking heavily, albeit more sporadically. According to Paul's grandmother the material conditions in the home were dreadful, with Paul sleeping in soiled sheets and there not being any food in the house. Also, according to Nancy there had been regular fights between Sheila and Gerald.

Paul had continued to attend school fairly well but all the previous week had arrived late, alone and hungry, and had fallen asleep in class several times. He has seemed sad and withdrawn, according to his classroom teacher.

On this occasion, after an initial assessment, a strategy discussion was triggered and agreement reached to proceed with enquiries under Section 47 of the Children Act. A core assessment began and a child protection conference was subsequently convened. Even though Sheila seemed to want to work in partnership with the department, the continuing risk of significant harm to Paul seemed to merit this course of action.

An initial child protection conference was held and Paul was registered on the Child Protection Register under the category of neglect.

A social worker, Ellen Grey, was allocated to the case and she completed a core assessment. Paul went to stay with Nancy, his grandmother, again for a few weeks with his mother's agreement. The assessment had gone well and was nearing completion.

It looked likely that some kind of shared care arrangement between Sheila and Gerald and Nancy would be agreed. Paul would stay with his grandmother with a gradual return home monitored by the core group. An agreement about Nancy taking over his care during stressful periods was reached. A range of supportive services was put in place. Both parents were doing well and had cooperated fully throughout the assessment.

Two days ago, a distraught Nancy phoned to say that Sheila had been found dead that morning at home and it was thought she had died from asphyxiation due to alcohol consumption (commonly known as choking on one's own vomit).

Nancy felt that, although she was willing to carry on looking after Paul in the short term, she was worried about being able to manage everything she needed to do for him on her own on a permanent basis and also it was costing her a fortune.

Sheila's death has thrown the original plan into disarray. Ellen has to make some pressing decisions about Paul's placement, both in the short and longer term. An updated assessment will be required but urgent decisions need to be made in the meantime.

Ellen is torn between leaving Paul with his grandmother – as she feels that this is placing great stress on her (particularly at this sad time after her daughter's death) – and placing Paul with foster carers. She feels that Nancy is well intentioned in wanting to care for her grandson but is concerned about her age and health (she suffers from bronchitis and smokes heavily) and whether she will be able to meet Paul's needs in the longer term. Gerald is overwhelmed by grief and saying that he is going to change and do the right thing by his son. He wants Paul to come home to him. Ellen feels very pessimistic about Paul returning to his father in any permanent way given his past history of relapse.

Paul has been settled at his grandmother's. He has been more alert and responsive at school and seemed happier in himself while living there according to his class teacher.

Ellen decided to complete a decision tree in partnership with her colleague from the family support team who is also in the core group.

They decide to undertake the exercise in order to help them in their thinking about immediate plans for Paul and for the recommendations they will be making to the child protection review conference. The scores given in the decision tree do not indicate the 'right' decision but simply represent the colleagues' thinking about the likelihood and desirability of the various options. Ellen will be better able to explain her decisions and recommendations if she is able to understand her thinking and think through the options with a colleague.

1. The decision to be made is: Where will Paul live? Ellen thinks that care proceedings may need to be instigated for Paul, so that a decision about his future can be made properly – but decisions made about his immediate placement will have implications for the future.

Ellen has to make some quick decisions in partnership with colleagues and with Nancy and Gerald about whether to leave Paul in Nancy's care in the short term; but she also has to think ahead about whether there is any possibility of Paul remaining with Nancy in the long term and, indeed, if this would represent a good plan for Paul.

The options as far as Ellen can see them are as follows.

Option A Paul stays with Nancy with a view to carrying out a kinship assessment to see if Paul's needs will best be met by Paul remaining with Nancy in the long term.

Option B Paul moves to short-term foster carers with a view to seeking and assessing permanent new carers for him, possibly through adoption.

Option C Paul stays with Nancy in the short term but with a view to a permanent new family being sought for him, possibly through adoption.

Option D Paul returns to his father's care with a view to this being a permanent arrangement.

Options A to D are now explored in more detail below.

Option A

This is the option that Ellen favours instinctively. She also knows that The Children Act (s23, para 2) encourages wider use of extended family placements. She believes that this option is likely to be the one with the best outcome. Nancy has a good and affectionate relationship with Paul and he is attached to her. Nancy has helped out in Paul's care for significant periods in the past. Although Ellen has some concerns about Nancy's ability to meet aspects of Paul's needs, such as when he grows into adolescence and some of his educational needs, she feels that a good kinship assessment would identify these areas with Nancy and a plan could be put in place to address these issues.

Ellen has spoken with Paul and he has indicated that he wishes to stay with his grandmother. She feels that this option would be least disruptive for Paul and it would enable him to have an ongoing relationship with his father – who, although Ellen feels is not able to provide satisfactory care for Paul, still has an affectionate relationship with him. Ellen is mindful too of messages from research which (although there is limited evidence from UK research to date) suggest that kinship care is a viable option for long-term care for children, particularly where there is a desire for continued parental contact. Broad and others (2001) in an in-depth study of kinship care in one London Borough, found a significant pattern of 'mid- to long-term stability', which Broad (2004) argues:

> suggests that kinship care goes some way to fulfilling the UK's key child welfare policy aims of reducing the number of placement moves for children looked after, improving placement stability and a child's sense of emotional permanence.

Many of the negative indicators for kinship care relate to poverty, lack of support and training but Ellen feels that there is good support available for kinship carers within her department.

Ellen and her colleague identify three possible consequences of this placement and give a high score to the likelihood of the placement being successful.

Option B

Ellen knows that there are some arguments for a decisive approach to permanency planning, recognising that Nancy is under stress and grieving and will not be in a position to meet Paul's immediate needs and that, in the longer term, it might be better to look at all Paul's needs and seek a family who can meet them all. With this model, Nancy could be considered as a prospective permanent carer if she wished. In theory, short-term carers would be able to assist in the process of assessing Paul's needs and preparing him for permanent placement. Ellen knows that the available research tends to suggest that outcomes for children placed in successful adoptive placements are good, although this is tempered by the difficulties of finding adoptive parents as children (especially boys) get older or if they have special needs. She also knows that contact with birth and extended family is less likely to survive if children are placed for adoption.

Ellen's experience of placing children within her own authority lead her to feel that the chances of a good match with Paul for short-term carers is chancy at best; and that the likelihood of recruiting suitable permanent carers within a reasonable time period is low. Ellen doesn't feel that the placement is 'highly likely' to break down but thinks it is a possibility. She feels pessimistic about the chances of this option leading to a successful transition to a permanent new family; and thinks the likelihood of the short-term placement drifting into a long-term one is high. She therefore scores the consequences accordingly.

Option C

Ellen does not favour this option – of leaving Paul with Nancy in the short term with a view to seeking alternative permanent carers – as she believes this option would be stressful all round. She scores highly the likelihood of a permanent new family not being found and the placement drifting into permanence in an unplanned way. This would mean that the proper kinship assessment would be unlikely to be carried out; and a proper plan to identify Paul's needs and Nancy's capacity to meet them, and the support required to bring this about, would also not be made.

Option D

Ellen is pessimistic about Paul returning to live with his father. Gerald has had significant problems with alcohol over a long period. Sheila was the main carer for Paul and it was only through her efforts that any stability existed, at times, in the family home. Gerald's medical prognosis is poor. He is likely to die if he does not give up drinking but there is no suggestion, based on previous experience, that he would have success in giving up alcohol. Ellen feels that Paul is wary around his father and, although he is pleased to see him for short periods, always seems happy to return to Nancy afterwards. Ellen scores the likelihood of placement breakdown highly and feels that, even if the placement could be maintained, it would be erratic and problematic and would be unlikely to meet Paul's needs.

Scoring the options

Once the likelihood scores are all recorded, Ellen and her colleague place the desirability scores next to each of the consequences. These are largely based on their practice values and experience. Once the calculations have been made, the option that emerges as the most favourable is the option of Paul staying with Nancy whilst a kinship assessment for prospective permanent care is carried out (Option A).

The fact that this option 'won out' may not come as a great surprise. One might ask: what is the point of undertaking an exercise which identifies the option that was favoured in the first place? But carrying out the process has forced Ellen to weigh up the options; discuss them with a colleague; think through the research evidence; and balance this with her knowledge of the child and family and normal practice within her own authority. It has offered her the opportunity to take a step back and come up with considered recommendations. It might prevent a knee-jerk reaction to the catastrophe that has occurred within the family; and this process will enable her to articulate her thinking to various stakeholders. This process does not replace the normal decision-making process within the local authority. If Paul is received into the care of the local authority, the normal Looked After Children decision-making process will take place – but having done the exercise will help Ellen to argue for her chosen option by explaining why she favours one option over others.

Decision tree: Paul

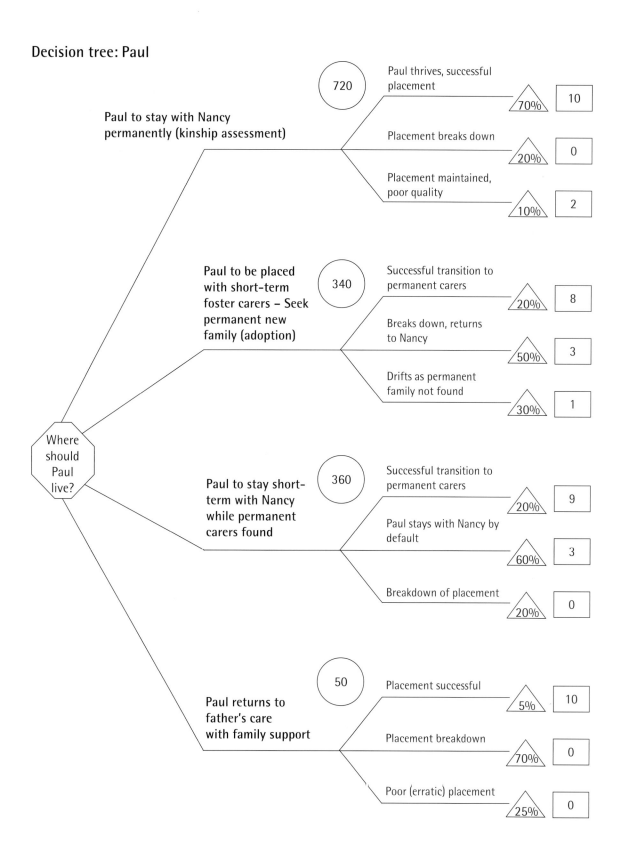

Paul to stay with Nancy permanently (kinship assessment)

720

Paul thrives, successful placement — 70% — 10

Placement breaks down — 20% — 0

Placement maintained, poor quality — 10% — 2

Paul to be placed with short-term foster carers – Seek permanent new family (adoption)

340

Successful transition to permanent carers — 20% — 8

Breaks down, returns to Nancy — 50% — 3

Drifts as permanent family not found — 30% — 1

Where should Paul live?

Paul to stay short-term with Nancy while permanent carers found

360

Successful transition to permanent carers — 20% — 9

Paul stays with Nancy by default — 60% — 3

Breakdown of placement — 20% — 0

Paul returns to father's care with family support

50

Placement successful — 5% — 10

Placement breakdown — 70% — 0

Poor (erratic) placement — 25% — 0

Practice development session 9: Decision tree

Aims

To explore the application of decision theory, including the decision tree, to decision-making with children and families; and to test out this approach in relation to participants' own practice.

Method

■ Introduce the ideas about decision theory using Presentation 2 slides 14–18 (see Appendix or Download from www.ncb.org.uk/resoures/support) and the notes on Decision theory and Different schools of thought (pages 101–102).

   Note: If the group has not already covered the intuitive–analytical debate in an earlier session, then include some of the material on Intuition and Analysis (pages 10–11) and some of the earlier content from Presentation 2 here.

■ Ask participants the following questions.

   – How do these ideas relate to your own experiences of making decisions with children and families, particularly during assessment?

   – How would you describe your own decision-making processes?

   – Does anyone here use tools or a specific approach?

   – Would you be interested in a tool that would help you become more analytical and structured in your approach?

Introduce the decision tree, using the following steps.

■ Use the notes in the section above to explain the purpose and potential uses of decision trees. Distribute the blank decision tree and instructions (page 104).

■ Use a case study (such as Decision tree on page 105) to talk through how a tree may be completed. It would be useful to run through a previously completed tree (such as Decision tree).

■ Invite participants to form groups with no more than six per group.

■ Ask participants in each group to volunteer cases where a crucial decision needs to be made or has recently been made. Then invite each group to agree on which one to use for this exercise.

■ Invite each group to work together on the completion of a decision tree for the case they have chosen. Tell them that they will have 20–30 minutes to complete it.

■ Reconvene the full group, but tell the participants to sit with the members of their small groups.

■ Invite the small groups to give brief feedback to the full group on: the decision that was under consideration; the options considered; the possible consequences; and how (or whether) they reached a decision and agreement on the option that provided the most desirable outcome.

- Ask the small groups whether they reached consensus easily; what factors they took into consideration when weighing up options; and how much they drew on research evidence, practice experience and so on.

- Ask the small groups whether they made the decision they think they would have made if they had not used this method and, if so, whether doing the exercise using the decision tree would help in explaining or justifying their decision.

- Ask participants to consider what potential uses the decision tree might have. Answers could include, for example, training, supervision, and providing justification for decisions to managers.

Recording and reporting

This section will consider key research and practice messages relating to the recording and reporting of information gathered during assessments. The assessment report is only one part of the child's record, although it is an important marker of how far the practitioner had developed their understanding of the child and family situation at a particular point in time. Whilst this toolkit has drawn on research, inspection reports and messages from serious case reviews regarding the quality of assessment reports, there are some more general messages to be learnt regarding the overall quality of recording and reporting which will help to inform analysis. We will examine current and forthcoming issues affecting recording timescales, the principles and common pitfalls of recording, the importance of chronologies to safeguarding children plus finally reaching conclusions and report writing. The practice tool associated with this section is a checklist for critical thinking and report writing.

Current issues regarding recording timescales

In the case of assessments undertaken within the *Framework for Assessment of Children in Need and their Families* (Department of Health and others 2000), the timescales that accompany the framework have in recent years provided the cut-off point that determines at what stage an assessment is viewed as being completed. Recently, however the Munro review of child protection (2011) called on the government to:

> remove the distinction between initial and core assessments and the associated timescales in respect of these assessments replacing them with the decisions that are required to be made by qualified social workers when developing an understanding of children's needs and making and implementing a plan to safeguard and promote their welfare.

In their response to the review (2011), the government has acknowledged that:

> targeted timescales for assessment have distorted the focus onto one small part of a child's journey rather than the whole journey from needing to receiving help.

They have announced an intention to move away from prescriptive timescales and focus instead on timeliness, quality of assessment and effectiveness of help. The lessons from pilots undertaken throughout 2011 in around nine local authorities will inform the development of new guidance, which is likely to appear in 2012.

Many practitioners will welcome these changes. Some of those involved in the Putting analysis into assessment project commented that they did not feel that they were in a position to draw conclusions, with the level of clarity that was expected of them within the 35 day time limit for core assessments. We mentioned in the introduction the frustration that practitioners often express at having to fit complex and rapidly changing information into an IT system that can seem to work against rather than promote the development of a meaningful narrative.

There is a need for caution, however, as few would want to return to the unfocused, lengthy assessments that were more commonplace pre 2000 when the Orange Book (Department of Health 1988) was one of the few assessment tools available. The challenge in the coming months will be to seek to loosen the more rigid and restrictive aspects of the existing system and promote meaningful interaction between practitioners, children and their families, while at the same time achieving focused, systematic, analytical practice that supports timely decision-making and ensures that children receive effective help to improve their outcomes.

Recording

Most practitioners would agree that whatever the frustrations involved in recording, maintaining an accurate and up to date record is an essential part of the social work task. Again and again child death inquiries and serious case reviews highlight the role of poor quality record keeping across all agencies as a contributory factor (Victoria Climbie 2003, Peter Connelly 2009, Ryan Lovell Hancox 2011).

The only 'assessment' completed involved the writing down of limited and sometimes contradictory information provided by Kouao (Laming 2003). In fact recording is an essential tool for all aspects of social work but especially for being able to make informed judgements about needs and risk of harm and for analysing the interplay of different factors on influencing potential outcomes for children. Walker, Shemmings and Cleaver (2003) identified the purpose of recording as:

■ supporting effective partnerships with users and carers

■ assisting continuity when workers are unavailable or change

■ providing a documented account of a department's involvement with an individual service user

■ providing evidence for planning and allocating resources at an individual and strategic level

■ facilitating reflection, analysis and planning

■ supporting supervision and professional development

■ recording that the practitioner and agency have met the expected standards of social care.

In the same publication (an interactive computer based training pack called Write Enough www.writeenough.org.uk), they also identify eight common pitfalls in recording:

■ case records are out of date

■ the child is missing from the record

■ facts and professional judgements are not distinguished in the record

■ the size of the record makes it difficult to manage

■ there is no assessment on record

■ the record is not written for sharing

■ the record is not written as a tool for analysis

■ the record is disrespectful to the service user.

Case records are out of date

It continues to be a challenge for social workers to balance their time appropriately between face-to-face work and keeping an accurate and up-to-date record. The record is integral to practice and to the service users and carers as well as to all the professionals involved in decision-making with and for children. Inadequate recording can mean that decisions are not based on robust evidence. Walker and others (2003) highlighted that most practitioners are unaware of how much time is needed for recording and they suggest that practitioners plan protected time and space for recording and that records are updated contemporaneously rather than saving information up in the head or allowing important information to accumulate.

The child is missing from the record

This depressing finding is one that appears again and again and whilst children appear in records, their own voices and their wishes and feelings are often missing, giving the impression that they have not been a part of the assessment. The reasons why this happens are explored more fully in the section Involving children but the result can be decisions being made that do not reflect a true picture of the child and their concerns. It is helpful to see children alone, plan the time needed to enable children to communicate, and represent children's views in their own voices and ensure that children's views are clearly marked in files (see page 71–81).

Facts and professional judgements are not distinguished in the record

Problems arise when observed and verified facts are not differentiated from opinion. Strongly expressed opinions, or views that concur with the social workers can end up being recorded as fact. Opinions are often stated, but not then substantiated, or early opinions can influence the later management of cases and that important information can be overlooked as a result of this tendency. Walkers and others (2003) recommend recording facts first followed by an analysis of them and they urge practitioners to show where they have used research evidence in their analysis.

The size of the record makes it difficult to manage

Prior to computerised records this issue tended to be about having numerous overstuffed paper files to wade through when trying to establish the child's story, but now the issue tends to be about being able to navigate and understand the recording system. Other issues that impact on the size of the record are practitioners writing too much in an unfocused way and writing defensively. Walker and others (2003) suggest maintaining a focus, recording significant information and identifying its significance. Include a clear plan, maintaining the record regularly and cross-referencing where possible rather than duplicating information.

There is no assessment on file

Since the birth of computerised records and timescales it is much less likely that once an assessment has been decided upon that it won't take place. However, well-gathered information without an analysis does not constitute an assessment. In addition to ensuring that assessments on file are up to date, practitioners should ensure that the assessment has been shared with family and that closing and transfer summaries include evaluations of progress made and the effectiveness of interventions and that the assessment findings inform future plans.

The record is not written for sharing

Although many documents and reports are now routinely shared with service users, for example child protection conference reports and reports for reviews, user access to files has been regarded with a high level of suspicion by some practitioners. (This attitude can be compared to attitudes towards family involvement in conferences prior to this becoming the norm.) A number of actions to support family inclusion can be taken, such as using plain language, sharing copies of recording policies, sharing drafts of assessments, providing final copies of reports, sharing recording in an ongoing way and encouraging the family to contribute to the record

The record is not written as a tool for analysis

The case file is important to decision-making, so it should be more than a complex diary of the practitioner's actions and the responses of the service user. In order to use recording as a tool for analysis practitioners need to record not just **what** is happening but **why** and use genograms, ecomaps and chronologies to help in organising and analysing the information, as well as case summaries and current research to assist in evaluating interventions.

The record is disrespectful to the service user

For the practitioner the case record will be just one of a number of similar records they keep, but for the service user it is their record. The most obvious way in which the record may be disrespectful to the service user is in the way in which it is written. Failing to differentiate between fact and professional opinion, unsubstantiated opinions and oppressive or discriminatory statements may indicate that the practitioner is not thinking about how the record may affect the service user should they read the file. Practitioners should ask themselves, 'What would I think if I was the service user and read that?' Practitioners should always take care to check out basic details such as dates of birth and spelling of names with parents and young people at an early stage.

The important points above that Walker, Shemmings and Cleaver make are that far from being a dry and irrelevant aspect of practice, maintaining the child's record properly is central to competent, transparent and inclusive practice. More detail and a series of interactive exercises can be found on the Write Enough website (www.writeenough.org.uk). Even if there isn't time to look at the website, practitioners can usefully ask themselves whether the records they keep conform more closely to the first or second list above and then reflect on what action they can take to address any issues arising from the exercise.

Chronologies

In 2010 Practice guidance written for the social work inspection agency (SWIA) for Scotland stated:

> *Chronologies have become one of the most talked about and least understood tools in modern Social work practice.*

In the same way that recording has often been under the spotlight in recent years chronologies have been discussed and promoted in formal guidance and literature as an essential social work tool.

In a recent Community Care online article (27/9/2010) Tink Palmer, chief executive of a sexual abuse awareness charity the Marie Collins foundation is quoted as saying that 'abuse and neglect is more preventable when good chronologies are kept' and that 'patterns in social history and behaviour can be detected and something which might appear insignificant in isolation can be identified as a key warning sign in context'.

Chronologies provide a 'back story' to the current period of involvement that an agency has with a child and their family. This is critically important because of what has happened in the past is of enormous relevance in understanding and making decisions about current circumstances. For example, if a woman in Scotland, who has had four children removed from her care sequentially over a period of years, due to her substance misuse, turns up at a London hospital in the later stages of pregnancy, the record of past involvement with her and her family will be hugely influential in helping professionals make decisions regarding the unborn child.

As in the case of recording, numerous child death inquiries and serious case reviews have identified that an improved chronology would have provided protection for children. For example, in a 2009 case in the Vale of Glamorgan, an 18-year-old male, with a history of sexual offences, was placed in an emergency foster placement with a family with two young children. He went on to rape one child and sexually assault the other. The director of the department apologised for the 'fundamental flaws' in practice that led to the boy being placed, without the foster carers or the placement service being provided with a chronology of previous incidents or the findings of previous assessments made regarding the risk he may pose to others.

Chronologies do more than provide a basic list of events; a good chronology is a tool for analysis, it can amongst other things:

■ provide early clues of troubling patterns

■ provide evidence of strengths and coping behaviours in the past

■ provide an understanding of how a parent's own childhood experiences may have impacted on their parenting capacity

■ help in understanding potential flashpoints or risky constellations of events for individuals and families

■ uncover connections and relationships within and across a family network

■ help in decision-making about the point when enough is enough in terms of attempts to change harmful behaviours

■ be a tool for building understanding in partnership with children and their parents

■ protect families from unfair decisions being made without recourse to background information.

There has been some confusion as to what should actually be contained within a chronology. According to an Integrated Children's system document: Analysing and recording significant harm (DCSF 2010), chronologies are a list of significant events not a list of case events. These are described as 'events relevant to an understanding of the case history and the child's current circumstances'. For example significant events may consist of both positive and negative events in the life of the family, such as births of children and early years of children's lives including parental attitudes, illnesses, accidents, periods of hospitalisation, deaths, house moves and changes in family make-up, educational progress and achievements. In addition to family information, the chronology should record all professional involvement with the family and the outcome of this, such as family support interventions, reports of domestic abuse, criminal investigations and offences and the results of these, child protection investigations, professional meetings and interventions and the family's response to these.

Taking the time to ensure that key information is entered into a chronology can be a challenge to practitioners who are already suffering from data entry fatigue. Some of the ICS recording systems are better than others at transferring information from the case file into a chronology, but few of the systems in use allow for a more in-depth chronology, beyond the simple recording of events, to be created. Steve Lidicott, ICS expert panel chair quoted in Community Care online (27/9/2010) said that: 'The expert panel on ICS have acknowledged that ICS has not achieved what it should have in terms of chronologies.' He added: 'it has made life more complicated in this area' and acknowledged that concerns had been noted from practitioners that the chronology functionality in the system is not adequate and does not allow them to create meaningful chronologies consisting of more than computer generated dates and event headings.

So for the time being many practitioners will need to rely on making their own chronologies and uploading these on to the IT system. Multi-agency chronologies are likely to need to be completed manually, through close negotiation with different agency representatives.

The SWIA guidance (Donnelly 2010) provides a useful checklist for a good chronology. It should be:

- a useful tool in assessment and practice

- a part of assessment, but not the full assessment

- a working tool that promotes engagement with people who use services

- an accurate, good, up-to-date case recording

- flexible, with detail collected that may be increased if risk increases

- be reviewed and analysed, a chronology that is not reviewed regularly is of limited relevance

- of sufficient detail, but not a substitute for recording in the file

- aware that different constructions of a chronology are needed for different reasons, for example current work and examining historical events

- aware that single agency and multi-agency chronologies set different demands and expectations

- a record of what was done at the time – many chronologies list events, dates, etc. but do not have a column that sets out the action that was taken at the time, this column should also include a note when there was no action.

Drawing conclusions and writing reports

The aim of this toolkit has been to put in place the right mental attitudes and practices to support analytical thinking throughout the assessment process. Routinely practising these skills of critical thinking should contribute to good report writing.

Establishing the agency's position and conclusions regarding the needs of children and their families should be an ongoing process of information-gathering; observations; checking out; reflection; consideration of evidence, research and theory as it relates to the case; and more besides.

So firstly, what does a practitioner need to consider in reaching their conclusions? For their own integrity, they will want their conclusions to be as fair, balanced and accurate as possible. They should therefore be clear that they have a good balance of information and a critical approach to making sense of it.

A useful checklist that identified the features for critical thinking was developed in an education toolkit from Antioch University (below). If practitioners can satisfy themselves that they are doing all of these things and they are able to demonstrate this in their writing they are likely to be well on the way to writing good analytical reports.

117

Individuals who routinely apply critical thinking in a range of life roles:

- analyse information and events objectively and develop verification processes

- discern cause and effect

- distinguish fact and opinion, influence and manipulation

- synthesise information and ideas

- seek to be well informed and take the total situation into account

- seek reasons

- judge the credibility of a source, using credible sources and accurately crediting sources

- are open minded

- ask questions for clarification and challenge

- deduce and induce and make judgements of their deductions and inductions

- make and judge value judgements

- identify assumptions.

Taken from: Keene, NH (1999) The Critical Skills Program, Antioch University, New England. *Education by Design Coaching kit Level 2.*

In putting the above into practice when reaching conclusions, practitioners should have gathered and be ready to present information that both supports and disputes their original, emerging and most recent hypotheses; and include the perspectives of all relevant parties, family members and professionals. Where there are disagreements in perspectives, the practitioner should resist the temptation to use language that undermines one point of view and amplifies another.

It is important and can be helpful to remember that a practitioner's conclusions are theirs alone. They neither have a crystal ball, nor do they know everything there is to know about the past, present or the likely future. The practitioner can, therefore, only seek to provide a well thought-out weighing up of what they do know; and, if done fairly, honestly, highlighting strengths and weaknesses, avoiding stereotypes, unfair assertions and denigrating language, they should not be able to stray too far from the 'truth' as they know it.

The practitioner's conclusions should draw on a wide view of the family's circumstances, being careful not to overlook or minimise the significance of social and environmental factors, such as people's experience of poverty or discrimination. The practitioner should acknowledge the impact of power imbalances which affect the relationship they have with family members. Holland (2004), citing Sheppard and others (2001) puts forward the following characteristics, which should be features of conclusions.

Conclusions should be forward looking and solution focused. They should give due consideration to answers to the questions: What, from the past, can be built on? What is indicating itself as helpful or protective? What needs to happen to encourage this? To what extent can we find overlap in ours (the practitioner's) and the families' goals and harness this? Conclusions should also be flexible to both the changing circumstances of families and the changing needs of children over time. They should be balanced and integrate the views of service users.

When it comes to the practitioner reporting on their conclusions, it is important and only fair to service users that they provide an account of the decision-making process, explaining what they looked for, weighed up and how they reached the conclusions they did.

The report should of course be placed in context as to why the practitioner is involved; what the level and nature of their involvement with the family has been; and where, when and how many times they have seen the parents, child and so on. They should also refer to who they have consulted. The practitioner should also be explicit about any research that has informed their thinking, and the tools they have used to elicit views and facts, including describing how they have worked with children to involve them in the process.

The importance of the use of language in the report along with the ordering of points should not be underestimated. Even fairly innocuous-seeming words, such as 'claims' when applied to parents, when 'said' or 'stated' is being used for professionals' views, implies a different valuing of the information they are giving. It is important for the practitioner to be conscious of this, particularly given the pressure to 'make a case' in the, unfortunately, often adversarial court arena. Similarly, the practitioner must be careful not to always start with the negative when describing parents or children, which can have the impact of undermining any positives or strengths that are explored later. If negative facts or risks are described fairly, accurately and illustratively, they should speak for themselves and their importance be acknowledged in the final analysis – so their potency will not be reduced by acknowledging the positive things, such as a family's honesty or proactiveness in seeking their child's return home.

Finally, there should be an acknowledgement that people are not fixed in their behaviour; and an exploration of a parent's capacity for change and the prognosis for desired changes to occur should be explored. Recommendations that result from the assessment should be clearly stated with targets set where applicable, spelling out clearly what changes need to occur and by when.

When looking at one's own or others' reported conclusions, it may be useful to have the following questions in mind.

- Have the views of the relevant family members been established and integrated accurately and fairly?

- Is the view that is presented balanced; with a weighing up of positive factors, strengths and resilience factors alongside risks of harm and unmet needs?

- Is it clear how the decision was made? Has the process been made explicit? This includes not only the final decision-making process but also how the assessment was carried out, for example in terms of numbers of visits and who was consulted.

- Is there anything about the use of language that is unnecessarily loaded or undermining? Are there stereotypes or pathologising language in evidence?

- To what extent does the ordering of points impact on the way the report is received or understood? Are family members tending to be portrayed at first negatively?

The reflective questions above will help when reviewing reports and the practice tool on page 120. Barratt and Hodson (2006) also provide a useful checklist for evidence-based report writing, emphasising the activities that need to occur at each of the three stages: prior to writing, drafting and finally writing up the report.

Practice tool 10: Writing effective reports

Prior to writing a report

- Know the relevant theory/research

- Identify assumptions you bring into the situation

- Hypothesise prior to gathering information

- Gather information from a wide variety of sources

When drafting the report

- Sort information into appropriate categories/dimensions

- Acknowledge sources of information (including theory and research) and use research evidence appropriately

- Summarise each category

- Use summaries to test/form hypothesis

- Identify any gaps in information

- Use diagrams to sketch relationships between factors within and across the domains and dimensions of the assessment framework

- Use the idea of identifying processes that are linear or circular

- Use the idea of indentifying processes that lead to patterns of impairment/difficulty or strengths/benefits

- Use the following considerations as a checklist: intrusiveness, pervasiveness, modifiability, frequency, duration, unusualness

Writing

- Write the analysis so that it is a clear explanation of the situation with reasons (i.e. it shows your reasoning)

- Justify/substantiate your professional judgements

- Identify any gaps in knowledge/understanding and further action required

- Show that you have been reasonable and fair

- Ensure use of persuasive language does not undermine the views of parents, carers and children

- Reach a conclusion – compare and discriminate between the different choices that could be made

- Put your conclusions into action by writing a plan

Adapted from: Barratt and Hodson (2006) *Firm Foundations: A practical guide to organisational support for the use of research evidence*, Research in Practice.

Case study: Conclusions and reporting

Name	Age	Ethnicity	Role
Malcolm Bradley	39	White Irish	father
Jenny Bradley	41	White Irish	mother
Selina Bradley	15	White Irish	daughter
Glen Bradley	12	White Irish	son
Beatrice Bradley	3	White Irish	daughter

The school referred the above family to social services originally because they have been worried about Glen. He has been increasingly aggressive and argumentative in school recently. He is a very able child, but seems apathetic and not to be concentrating or applying himself to his work as much as he did until just a few months ago. He has also been bullying younger children.

Malcolm agrees that there has been a deterioration in Glen's behaviour and says that Glen has been very hostile towards him and takes no notice of him most of the time. Malcolm was made redundant 6 months ago and has been drinking fairly regularly in the day and more than usual.

Jenny has had several periods of depression over the years and seems to be exhibiting feelings of paranoia and anxiety recently. When asked about how she was feeling recently she said 'probably like my mum' and stared into space. Malcolm told the social worker that Jenny's mother disappeared when she was three years old and that at the moment she seems quite preoccupied with this.

Selina has moderate learning disabilities and the special school she attends are concerned that she is increasingly exhibiting sexualised behaviour towards male teachers and some pupils. When this was raised gently with Selina she had a giggling fit. Her parents did not seem very worried as they thought it natural for her to be inquisitive about her body and those of others at her age. They did not seem very comfortable about the idea of talking with Selina about sex and said they have avoided doing so up to now.

Beatrice is slightly overweight and a very placid child. Jenny seems very reluctant for anyone to look after Beatrice other than her and is quite anxious about her, often wondering without cause (in the GP's view) if Beatrice has various illnesses or disabilities. The health visitor has been quite concerned about Jenny's anxiety in relation to Beatrice.

Jenny also seems to have become quite obsessive about cleaning recently, repeatedly scrubbing and polishing the same areas within less than an hour of doing it. Jenny does not work and hasn't for several years.

Within practice development 9 there is an opportunity to develop this case study and to practise forming and wording conclusions that are in line with the principles discussed earlier.

Practice development session 10: Conclusions and reporting

Aim

To reflect on how conclusions are reached, what they should 'look like' and how they are reported on; and to provide participants with an opportunity for peer feedback and to test out ideas in practice.

Activity 1

Method

- In advance of the session, you could ask each participant to bring an assessment report (ideally an initial assessment, as a core assessment would take longer to read). Remove any references to the subjects of the reports (i.e. make them anonymous).

- Mark the reports in a way that will ensure that you do not give the report back to the author for the activity itself. Staple two blank sheets of paper to the back of each report.

- Give a ten-minute presentation about conclusions and reporting using presentation 9 slides 85-88 plus also drawing on points made in the narrative section above.

- After the presentation, invite questions and discussion of any issues it raises for participants.

- Invite participants to form pairs.

- Give out the assessments, trying to ensure that no one gets their own.

- Ask the pairs to look at each of the assessments. Ask them to look with a (supportively) critical eye and ask themselves the following questions:

  - Is the child visible? Are their needs identified?
  - Is there evidence of theory and research in the assessment?
  - Are the domains and their interrelationship clearly articulated?
  - Is the decision-making process thinking/weighting of issues apparent?
  - Are cultural issues addressed?
  - Is it clear what needs to happen and how change will be measured?

- Invite each pair of participants to record two points that are positives; and two that are suggestions for how the assessment could have been strengthened – particularly from an analytical perspective. (Making four points in all.)

- Ask the pairs to pass the assessments on to another pair (still trying to ensure that no one has their own) and repeat the exercise.

- Collect in the assessments and then pass each to its owner (author).

- Ask the participants to read all the comments and reflect on them; then to discuss with their partner whether the comments are helpful and might strengthen their future practice.

- Ask for two or three volunteers to briefly summarise their assessment and read out the comments, stating how the comments might have helped them. Stress that there are lots of reasons for people not being able to do everything that the theory tells them is good practice – so urge people not to feel too defensive.

■ To round off the activity, allow time for participants to share any thoughts that have arisen from receiving such feedback on their report.

Activity 2

Method

Divide the group into smaller groups of three or four.

■ Ask each small group to come up with a set of conclusions and recommendations, either for a case that one of them has been working on or (imaginary conclusions) for Case study: Conclusions and reporting (distributing the case study if necessary).

■ Stress that they should take care to ensure that their conclusions are: forward looking, balanced, flexible to changing circumstances, and that the views of service users are considered and integrated. And also that they consider their use of language and ordering of points.

■ Ascribe different roles to the members of the small group for a role-play exercise. Choose one member of each group to be the social worker or team manager who is going to tell the 'recipient' their conclusions and recommendations, including how they were reached.

■ Choose one or two members of each group to be the recipients of the information. If using the case study, the recipients might be: Jenny, Malcolm, one of the children, the referrer, health visitor, or someone from one of the schools.

■ Decide which member of the group will be the observer. Explain to them that they will watch the role-play and then be asked to give feedback on their observations afterwards.

■ Once roles are assigned and group members have formed a set of conclusions in their minds (notes may be taken), instruct the participants to role-play the social worker or manager giving the information to the agreed participants. Tell them they will have five minutes for this.

■ After five minutes (or longer if you feel it is needed) stop the role-play and invite feedback from those in each role, including observers.

■ If time permits, swap the roles around, changing the recipient's identity, and repeat the role-play.

■ Invite feedback about the role-play, asking to what extent people were able to be forward looking, for example, or to explain the decision-making process.

Reviewing decisions: Critical decision method

When we talk about reviewing decisions in this context we mean reflecting on decisions as a source of learning as opposed to reviewing as part of the formal statutory process. We have identified a technique that we have used and has proven to be helpful as a reflective exercise. This story-based approach was first put forward by Gary Klein (Klein 2000). Klein belongs to the naturalistic school of decision theorists. His approach is to look for what can be learnt from the patterns and stories that emerge from examining a wide range of different decision-making situations. In his book, *Sources of Power: How people make decisions* (2000), he suggests that we organise our cognitive world – the world of ideas, concepts, objects and relationships – by linking the various parts into stories. He proposes that by understanding how this happens, we can learn to make better use of the power of stories.

Klein suggests that a story is a blend of several ingredients:

- **agents** – the people who figure in the story

- **predicament** – the problem the agents are trying to solve

- **intentions** – what the agents plan to do

- **actions** – what the agents do to achieve their intentions

- **objects** – the tools the agents will use

- **causality** – the effects, both intended and unintended, of carrying out the actions

- **context** – the many details surrounding the agents and actions

- **surprises** – the unexpected things that happen in the story.

Klein proposes that a great deal can be learnt from the analysis of stories and that – whilst this is not scientific because the conditions cannot be controlled – it is possible for people hearing a story being told, to learn about motivation, intentions, pick up some ideas and fathom some of the mysteries.

Klein believes a story records an event that happened within a natural context, and in a way is a report of an experiment, linking cause and effect. It says 'under these conditions this is what happens'; and Klein suggests that we like stories because they are like reports of research projects, only easier to understand, remember and use.

He gives the example of jurors in a trial and how they make sense of the evidence. The decision-makers (jurors) try to assemble the facts into a story because the task of holding all the evidence in their heads without this is too difficult.

Klein suggests that story telling can help in making a diagnosis. In troubleshooting a piece of equipment, a technician can build a story of what might have gone wrong to explain a set of observed symptoms. Klein suggests that if troubleshooting and stories are viewed in the same way, we can apply the criteria of good stories to get a sense of how troubleshooting proceeds. The troubleshooter is trying to detect a causal chain that leads from the initial conditions to the fault. By developing different explanations of what might be happening and then using this to gather more information the technician is undertaking a method of problem solving, both using the current state of knowledge and modifying it or building on it to move forward to diagnosis.

Klein suggests that stories are the most powerful method he has found for eliciting knowledge.

He suggests that if you ask experts to tell you what makes them so good at their job they will give general, non-specific answers but if you get them to tell you about tough cases – non-routine events where their skill made the difference – you will have a pathway into their perspective. Klein calls this method of eliciting information **The Critical Decision Method**, because it focuses attention on the key judgements and decisions that were made during an incident being described.

Klein uses an example of a piece of work undertaken by his team that involved one of his evaluators talking to a group of neonatal nurses and asking them how they spotted the early signs of sepsis (septic infection). They told her it was a mixture of intuition and experience. It was only when the evaluator listened to all the stories that experienced nurses told of what exactly they observed, that she could draw up a master list of clues to sepsis.

This toolkit will relate Klein's Critical decision method to the assessment of children and families in social work. The approach of story telling forms the basis of a framework for helping practitioners to reflect on the decisions made during the progress of a child's case through the system. This framework is designed to help practitioners in their analysis, understanding and consequently in their explanation of what influenced the various decisions. The method is not so much seen as a way of developing checklists that can be applied in other situations, as an attempt to build knowledge and understanding that could aid personal and professional development and be articulated within a team or across agencies and in reports.

The method that Klein uses with his team is to first of all find a good story; one with lots of expertise, perceptual skills and judgements. These aren't necessarily the dramatic stories, because often in those extremely dramatic situations there hasn't been the need to make subtle judgements and difficult decisions, as they tend to lead to rapid intuitive decisions. The stories they preferred were non-routine, complex stories where a novice might have faltered. The team developed a strategy for conducting interviews with practitioners and eliciting the information in a consistent way that allowed for the maximum reflection.

The method described by Klein is to make four passes through a story.

Pass 1   Ask for brief telling of the story to see if it has good possibilities and to identify the important parts so as not to waste time on trivialities.

Pass 2   A full telling of the story, pinning the details down to a timeline to get a better sense of what happened and to visualise (in a diagram) when things occurred and how long they took. If possible, the diagram identifies where one stage of knowledge transformed into another.

Pass 3   Revisit the story and probe the thought processes. Ask the person to answer the following questions.

- At what points did you change your assessment of the situation?

- What alternative goals may have existed at certain points?

- What other courses of action were available to the ones taken?

- What factors might have led to the chosen option?

- Ask hypothetical questions, such as what might have happened here if a particular piece of information had not arrived or if another agent in the story had acted in a different way?

- If a particular option had been blocked, what would their reaction have been?

- What would they have done or thought if something that happened hadn't happened?

- What might their assumptions have been?

Pass 4   Klein suggests that at each choice or decision point, you ask: Would a novice get confused? What mistakes could they make? Why would they make them?

Further to Klein's suggestions, ask the questions: what would be the possible consequences of a different decision; or if certain factors came into play at the different decision points? Then reflect on what has been learnt from completing the timeline.

In Klein's team they take a long time to learn how to undertake these interviews and gather the right information, probe the right areas and spot when expertise comes into play. For this toolkit, however, the technique needed to be developed into an exercise that could be:

■   undertaken by an individual practitioner to aid their own reflection

■   used by a team manager in supervision to help a practitioner reflect on a case

■   undertaken as a peer-development exercise in pairs

■   facilitated in a team-development session, either by an external facilitator or a team member, to aid team learning.

As part of the Putting analysis into assessment project, individual practitioners ran through the exercise a number of times; and several practitioners ran through their stories with team colleagues present. Practitioners commented that unpicking the stories in this way helped them to understand how their own values and assumptions often influenced the decisions they made; and it also helped them to recognise when they were drawing on experience, theory or research findings to inform their own decision-making.

One practitioner was particularly struck by how strongly his many years' experience of working with a substance-misusing parent led to a set of unconscious assumptions, which directed many of his actions.

Another practitioner was alarmed to realise that, despite a mentally ill mother she was working with being from a very different cultural background, she has almost overlooked this in the context of looking at the impact of the mental health issues on the mother–child relationship.

In one session with a whole team, a practitioner demonstrated how her own refusal to be drawn into the hysteria within and around a particular family enabled the child's need to remain central to decision-making.

The practice tool presented here is a template for logging the decision points on a timeline and contains a number of trigger questions to ask to promote reflection.

Practice tool 11: Critical decision tool

Stage 1 Write a very brief, broad, brush-stroke outline of the overall situation, no more than two or three lines. Consider whether this is a promising story for using in the exercise. Does it have examples of expertise, perceptual skills and judgements?

Stage 3 At each of the decision points ask some or all of the following questions.

- What factors influenced the decision? (e.g. research theory, resources, pragmatic considerations)

- Note points when you changed your understanding of the situation and say why.

- Note when a decision changed the direction of the story. How did this impact on your thinking and actions?

- What alternative goals may have existed at certain points?

- What courses of action were available other than the ones taken?

- What factors may have led to the chosen option?

- What might have happened at certain points if a particular piece of information had not arrived or if another agent in the story had acted in a different way?

- If a particular option had been blocked, what would your reaction have been?

Stage 2 Log decision points on the line; and note on this side what they were and when they were made. Include decisions made by other agents in the story as well as those made by you. Also include micro-decisions that may have impacted on the overall progress of the story

Stage 4
Revisit the decision points and ask if a novice could have got confused and made mistakes? Why would they have made them? Consider what the possible consequences of different decision and/or factors coming into play would be at the different decision points? Reflect on what the learning has been from completing the timeline.

Case study: Critical decision tool

Background information

Single mother with four children (two grown-up ones) with three different fathers, none of whom live with or have much contact with the family.

Maureen – mother (White Irish)

Paul – 17-year-old son (Mixed parentage – Irish/Black Caribbean)

Rosa – 11-year-old daughter (Mixed parentage – Irish/Indian)

Sarah-Jane – 9-year-old daughter (Mixed parentage – Irish/Indian)

Jason – 8-year-old son (Mixed parentage – Irish/Indian)

Sam – 5-year-old son (White/Irish). Exhibiting behaviour problems in school although is popular. CAMHS assessment – mild learning difficulty. Learning difficulty and behaviour holding him back.

Mum has a history of using social services to get financial help.

School concerned.

Maureen takes good care of the children generally/some mild depression.

Child psychologist had expressed concerns re. Sam being aggressive in the home.

Referral from school – Sam has a bruise on face allegedly caused by his brother Paul having hit him.

What factors influenced decisions?		Log decision points on the line; and note on this side what they were.
Previous knowledge of team		Unallocated.
Previously decided was 'child in need' (CIN). (Team and agency culture influence here.) Needed worker – good case for worker (Derek) to gain experience.		Allocated new social worker, Derek, for assessment of need.
Was first case for Derek and he wanted to explain to Maureen that there was a need to protect Sam but why it was not a Section 47 response. Also to observe.		Undertook joint visit with Linda (supervisor) (announced).
Maureen and Sam open to/willing for assessment. Influenced by Paul's age – adult. Treated as vulnerable young person.		Decision to see Sam and work directly with him.
Didn't need to challenge mum.		2nd visit – saw Paul and Sam separately and together.
'That's what we do' – bring everyone together to share knowledge, establish partnership working. Got school's perspective and get pupil referral unit and school talking – common aims. Increased school's understanding of Sam's home situation.		Thorough assessment of their home environment and knowledge about children's needs.
To prevent breakdown between mum and school. Belief in behaviourist approach.		Decision to hold network meeting. Mum invited.
Behaviour management. Anger, frustration about his father. Aim to help him recognise where anger comes from.		Decision for mum and school to communicate and use prizes and rewards to try and improve Sam's behaviour.
Thresholds/eligibility/politics/gate-keeping/Paul open about problems to Derek and willing to have counselling and thought he might work with them.		Refer Paul to counselling (will be a family consultation).
Wanted to encourage mum's independence (history of using services/getting to crisis). Low motivation due to depression and mum defining other priorities (e.g. losing weight).		(Adolescents team would not take because not mental health, so family approach required – Child and Family Consultation Service did take referral.)
Mum being quite positive.		Plans to refer mum to parent support group. Was a plan to refer mum to voluntary family support service for family work but mum not keen and not happening yet.
Importance of having an outlet. Build self-esteem. Positive effects on relationships at home. Divert from potential anti-social activities.		Decision to try and get all kids involved in more activities. 'Positive activities' programme.
Paul feeling a scapegoat. To build on network meeting, previous assessments, shift mum's description of Paul's problems.		Decision to encourage view of Paul as a role model. To try and encourage mum to use positive reinforcement, consistency.

[additional information]

First home visit met Mum and kids. Second visit met Paul.

Undertook core assessment.

Wanted to try and promote Mum's independence from SSD.

Decision to work with Sam and Paul directly because of nature of referral.

Network meeting – gave overall picture, discussed schooling and pupil referral unit.

House very tidy.

Children polite and well behaved. Paul friendly, polite, always there, articulate, agreed to go to counselling.

Relied on Mum's account. Sam gets in moods and Paul gets irritated.

Mum finds it difficult to get outside. House dark, curtains drawn, kids cooped up watching TV in four-bed flat.

Need opportunities after school and to get out.

Bruise was on head.

Bullying behaviour?

Mum open about it happening, cried at network meeting.

Paul upfront.

Referral made for Paul to go to counselling.

Anger towards his dad. Appreciated male figure (Derek) taking interest.

Sam took it hardest when his dad left (2 years ago).

Paul's dad not been around for years.

Mum previously distanced from children, gets very low and lacks self-esteem, comfort eats. Less likely to go out. On benefits.

School – put in various steps/measures.

Consistency between school and home in managing behaviour.

Educational psychologist recommended SEN statement.

Could a novice have made mistakes or different decisions? What would have happened?

- Worker was fairly inexperienced but well supervised. Without supervision, may have not seen whole picture.

- Worker was wondering at times what they were doing – sometimes difficult to see the wood for the trees.

- Agency team culture had a large part to play in route taken, i.e. keeping cases in CIN rather than in Section 47 if appropriate and possible.

- Family were open to intervention – different decision may have had to be taken if not.

- Saw the two children, Paul and Sam, separately as well as working with whole family – if hadn't taken this approach one part of system could have benefited without improvement in another, risk of problem reoccurring.

- The assessment of needs led to the identification of appropriate services. If needs not met, difficulties could have been compounded.

- Partnership approach – improvements in family relationships were noted and built on – if this approach not taken, family may have become demotivated.

- Ongoing support was available rather than pressure to close case – which may have led to problem reoccurring.

- Working on building networks of support to prevent isolation in future.

Practice development session 11: Critical decision tool

Aim

To introduce Klein's ideas about story telling as a method for reflecting on and understanding decisions; and to test out the critical decision method in practice.

Method

- In advance of the session, select two participants to use the Critical decision tool to talk through one of their cases. Ask them to choose, preferably, a case where an assessment is complete and which illustrates the complexity of decision-making. Ask them to write a brief summary paragraph, with basic factual information only, in advance of the session and to have copies to hand out at the session.

- Begin the session by asking participants if they feel they currently have time and opportunity to revisit case decision-making and to reflect, either alone or with colleagues, on how and why certain decisions have been made and what might have happened if these decisions had been different. If people feel they do have these opportunities then ask them to describe how, when what, with whom and so forth.

- Introduce Klein's work to the group with a brief presentation using the notes above (under 'Critical decision method').

- Distribute the blank critical decision timeline (page 127) and explain that this has been developed from Klein's ideas during the Putting analysis into assessment project.

- Suggest ways in which it might be used – for example, in a session such as this, for personal reflection, in co-working, in supervision, and in preparing reports for court – to organise thinking.

- Tell the group how two participants were invited to each write a paragraph on their cases before the session. Tell the group who the participants are.

- Stress to the group that the participants are very brave and thank them in advance for exposing their practice. Remind everyone to be positive and supportive in their questions.

- Have some prompt cards prepared, each with one of the following points written on it:
  - Research
  - Theory
  - Evidence of involvement of child
  - Evidence of partnership with parents
  - Interagency working
  - Hypothesising
  - Cultural review
  - Focus on needs
  - Checklists/resources

- Give out the cards so that each participant holds one.

- Ask the first presenting participant to introduce their case and hand out the summary.

- Make four passes through the case by doing the following.

    - Invite the participant to present a very brief summary.

    - Ask the participant to go though the case in more detail, identifying the decision points. Meanwhile, draw a timeline on the flip chart and add the decision points to it.

    - Revisit key decision points and ask the participant questions about their decisions and those of others, based on the trigger points on the critical decision sheet. Focus on trying to tease out as much as possible about influences, motivations, constraints, and unexpected developments. Invite other participants to ask questions, using their prompt card to focus their questions.

    - Go through the case one more time, asking whether less- or more-experienced practitioners might have behaved differently. Ask what effect this might have had.

- Encourage general discussion. If necessary, prompt the group with questions such as: Has the exercise raised particular issues? (Be sure to check that the presenting participants feel comfortable and not too exposed.) What does the practitioner learn from this exercise? What do others in the team learn? Do you feel that this would be a useful exercise to do when you are reporting on your assessments or preparing court reports? Would it be beneficial for you to do this on a regular basis with the team? Does it indicate to you a need for further training and development or other actions?

5. Team development activities

This chapter contains a range of resources for use by team managers or external facilitators during team meetings, on team away days or in practice development sessions, to assist in the development of a culture of reflection and analysis within the team. Apart from the peer review exercise these activities are not case specific; and are designed to open up discussion about analysis.

Activity 1: What is analysis?

Aim

To develop a shared understanding of what is understood by analysis.

> ### Objectives
>
> By the end of the activity participants will have:
>
> - expressed thoughts and ideas about analysis and how and when it takes place, who should be involved and how it relates to other elements of assessment
>
> - discussed a common understanding of the meaning of analysis
>
> - gained a common understanding of the definition of analysis and how it relates to judgement and decision-making.

Time

30–45 minutes.

Ideal numbers

Teams of between four and 12 (up to 20 if on a training course).

Method

- Invite the participants to form pairs.

- Give participants the What is analysis? Questions from page 136 (as a handout or write on a flip chart).

- Ask the participants, in their pairs, to discuss and answer the questions. Tell them they will have 15 minutes for this.

- When the 15 minutes are up, reconvene the full group.

- Ask for feedback from the group, taking each question in turn.

- Encourage a group discussion in which analysis' main components and facets are agreed.

Facilitator's notes

This exercise is a useful starting point for undertaking some exploration about the quality of analysis within a team, as it provides an opportunity to reflect together on what we mean by analysis. What you will tend to find is that analysis, in the participants' view, is made up of several components, which get drawn out and made explicit through the exercise. Also you will find that on training courses analysis means pretty much the same thing to most people, but there is a huge number of ways of describing it and different emphases on what is involved.

There is no 'right' answer to this exercise, although there could potentially be some wrong ones! Give out the following dictionary definition as a guide to the way participants should be thinking about analysis.

> The division of a physical or abstract whole into its constituent parts to examine or determine their relationship ... a statement of the results of this.
>
> *Collins Concise Dictionary*

And offer the following example of a wrong answer: 'information gathering' is not analysis nor is 'data management' but these are essential components.

What is analysis?

- What do you understand the word analysis to mean?

- What part does analysis play in assessments of need?

- How do you go about analysis – what does it involve?

- At what stage of an assessment do you analyse?

- Who might be involved in the analysis and how?

- How is analysis distinct from planning and decision-making?

- How does analysis contribute to planning and decision making?

Activity 2: SWOT analysis of the team's strengths and weaknesses

Aim

To provide a health check of analytical practice in the team and to develop action planning to address issues arising.

Objectives

By the end of the activity participants will have:

- reflected on the strengths, weaknesses, opportunities, and threats relating to their own personal practice

- reflected on the strengths, weaknesses, opportunities, and threats relating to the practice across the team as a whole

- had an opportunity to address any gaps and deficits

- articulated and recorded examples of the team's strengths and weaknesses in analysis

- identified actions to strengthen practice.

Time

1½–2 hours.

Ideal numbers

Any number, but if doing the activity with more than one team and breaking into groups, a total of no more than 24 people.

Method

- Draw a SWOT box, as shown below, on a flip chart or whiteboard.

Strengths	Weaknesses
Opportunities	Threats

- Using the following explanation, go through the SWOT analysis model and method. Explain that the method for completing the SWOT is to agree the following.

- **The strengths** – these are examples of how analytical practice is tangibly strong and positive, e.g. 'assessment reports commended by senior managers'.

- **Weaknesses** – where there are tangible deficits and weaknesses in practice, lack of confidence, competence, knowledge and skills, e.g. 'lack of use of evidence in reports'.

- **Opportunities** – what exists within the team, agency and wider environment, which will support the development of more analytical practice, e.g. 'PQ programme'.

- **Threats** – what factors create obstacles to the development of more analytical practice in the team, e.g. 'volume of work', 'timescales'.

■ Take each of the SWOT boxes in the order they appear above, asking the team members to shout out examples to place for each one. Record all suggestions in the box you are dealing with, unless they definitely fit into another category in which case they should be written down there. Continue until all the SWOT boxes are completed.

■ Tackle the next exercise either as the whole group or invite participants to form smaller groups. Revisit each area of the SWOT box and ask what needs to happen in the team (or agency) to support the strong areas and address the deficits. Record the participants' responses as a list of points.

■ Explain that the next task is to make the list of points practicable by identifying who will need to carry out each action; and by adding a timescale for when it should be completed. Ideally, any tasks arising from this exercise should be spread out amongst the team and not all ascribed to the team manager.

■ Encourage groups to log actions that they feel should be taken – even if they feel they are outside their scope. Encourage discussion and seek agreement about how these points can be fed into the wider organisation or even beyond, for example through a team manager or external networks.

■ The template below is useful for recording action planning.

Action	By whom	By when	Support/resources required	Outcome

Facilitator's notes

If the facilitator is the team manager, this exercise needs to be handled sensitively, allowing the team to come up with their own examples of strengths and weaknesses; whilst taking opportunities where appropriate to praise good practice and highlight weaknesses if the team don't come up with these themselves.

There is also a possibility that team members will wish to highlight deficits in management and supervision. One way to make this less personal is to divide the group into two or three smaller groups and give them a blank SWOT sheet to complete themselves and then put all the completed sheets on the wall. This will allow for acknowledgement of issues raised without it being too uncomfortable.

Activity 3: Scaling exercise

Aim

To ascertain how participants perceive their ability individually and as a team to undertake a thorough and balanced analysis.

Objectives

By the end of the activity participants will have:

- identified what helps and what hinders thinking analytically throughout an assessment; and how much the culture of their agency supports analysis

- discussed the use of a scaling system for demonstrating their responses to a number of questions about analysis

- gained a clearer picture of the perspectives and experiences of colleagues in relation to analysis as part of the assessment process.

Time

45 minutes to an hour.

Ideal numbers

4–16.

Method

- Make up ten separate cards with bold, clear numbers on (1–10), and lay them out in numerical order in a line on the floor, leaving sufficient space between them for a number of people to stand on one without spilling over onto the next.

- Tell participants that you will be reading out a series of statements and will want them to stand on the number that most accurately reflects their response, with 1 being completely disagree and 10 being completely agree.

- Read the first of the statements (see box over page).

> - The assessment framework helps practitioners to analyse information more systematically.
> - The culture in my team (or agency) supports reflective analytical practice.
> - I feel confident and competent in my knowledge of research and theory and in my ability to apply this to practice.
> - There are some areas of practice where I find it harder to use my analytical skills than others.
> - Developing a more analytical approach is pointless because you have to fit children's and families' needs into existing services in the end anyway.
> - Supervision helps me to develop a more analytical approach and be reflective.
> - I have a range of tools at my disposal to help in gathering information.
> - I have a range of tools at my disposal to help in analysing information.

- Ask participants to place themselves along the scale of 0–10, according to the extent to which they agree or disagree with the statement just read out.

- Ask those participants standing at the extreme ends of the scale why they have placed themselves there. Ideally, ask a couple of participants at each end and then ask those next to them until you reach the centre.

- Invite a couple of participants towards the bottom end of the scale (nearest '0') what would need to happen to enable them to move further up the scale. Ask people who are a little further towards the top end (nearer '10') as well.

- Allow around five to ten minutes altogether for discussion of the statement.

- Read the second statement in the box.

- Repeat the process (from 'Ask participants to place') until each statement in the box has been read out and acted upon.

- Round off the session by summarising what has been learnt from the exercise and highlighting interesting points.

Facilitator's notes

If there is fruitful discussion that carries on for longer over one point, you can reduce the number of statements. Take care not to let any one discussion go on for longer than ten minutes as the group's concentration will lapse (and they will get tired of standing up).

Depending on your reasons for undertaking this exercise, you may want to capture some of what is said, in which case it is a good idea to choose a scribe to make a note, as this exercise can lead to some interesting points being made by participants as to why they have placed themselves on a particular number.

Where there are obvious trends, with most people standing in roughly the same place, this provides useful information; as do the views of those who stand alone.

This exercise has always, without fail, led to a rich discussion – with a variety of views being expressed and points debated.

140

Activity 4: Self-assessment of undertaking analytical assessments

Aim

To enable practitioners to reflect in detail on the extent to which their current assessment practice reflects an analytical approach, and to consider the implications of this for a team's culture and practice.

Objectives

By the end of the activity participants will have:

- given detailed feedback on a number of questions relevant to their own analytical skills, reflected on the results of this is in pairs and discussed issues arising from the exercise within the wider group

- created an action plan for themselves to address any gaps or weaker areas in their own analysis.

NB: If this exercise is being undertaken with a whole team it can also be used to discuss any issues arising for the team, for example future policy and practice, practice development opportunities, development, shadowing and mentoring.

Time

1 hour 15 minutes.
Five minutes for ideas storm, 15–30 minutes to complete the self-assessment tool, followed by 15 minutes sharing in pairs and 15 minutes for discussion.

Ideal numbers

Everyone in the team. An even number of participants is required.

Method

- Ask participants what factors they think would indicate that an analytical approach to assessment practice was in place in a team. Write ideas on a flip chart as an ideas storm and discuss with the group. Depending on the suggestions, refer to the self-assessment tool (page 143) to fill in any gaps. Ask the group to indicate how well they think they do putting analytical assessment into their practice.

- Hand out the self-assessment tool and explain that participants should spend 15 minutes completing this on their own. Ask them to think carefully about the score they are giving themselves and make comments in the space provided on the form. Ask them not to complete the final question (14) until after the next stage.

- Ask people to pair up and go through their forms together, discussing their responses and giving each other feedback where appropriate about what they have observed about each other's practice and whether they would agree with each other's scores

- Ask participants to work in their pairs to complete the action plan points in question 14.

141

■ Bring the whole group back and ask for general feedback about the experience, and whether they learnt anything about their own practice from the process. Ask a few people to share an action in their action plan.

■ Ask the whole group (including the manager, if present) what issues the exercise brings up for the team as a whole and what kinds of actions the team might need to take to move towards more analytical practice. Make some helpful suggestions here, including: Can regular practice development sessions be timetabled? Are there opportunities for shadowing and mentoring? And, are other learning and development opportunities available?

Self-assessment of own work	
Thinking about your work as a whole and reflecting on recent reports you have completed, on a scale of 0–10 (0 = not at all well, and 10 = perfectly) how well do you think you?	
1. Break down the child(ren)'s needs and explore them in detail – consider the impact on outcomes, of different needs being met (or not).	0 1 2 3 4 5 6 7 8 9 10 Comments
2. Draw on and demonstrate knowledge of theory/research/formal knowledge in your reports.	0 1 2 3 4 5 6 7 8 9 10 Comments
3. Explore cultural/equality issues and issues of power, fully and clearly.	0 1 2 3 4 5 6 7 8 9 10 Comments
4. Demonstrate an open-minded approach to exploring different hypotheses/ explanations/understanding of the circumstances.	0 1 2 3 4 5 6 7 8 9 10 Comments
5. Provide a thorough analysis of the information gathered.	0 1 2 3 4 5 6 7 8 9 10 Comments
6. Demonstrate a creative approach to consulting with/involving the child(ren)	0 1 2 3 4 5 6 7 8 9 10 Comments
7. Articulate the way decisions or conclusions were reached, for example, describing different options and how they have been considered.	0 1 2 3 4 5 6 7 8 9 10 Comments
8. Demonstrate that other key professionals have been appropriately consulted with/involved in the work leading up to the preparation of the report.	0 1 2 3 4 5 6 7 8 9 10 Comments

9.	Show evidence of decisions/ recommendations having been discussed with child(ren), parents/carers/other key professionals.	0 1 2 3 4 5 6 7 8 9 10 Comments
10.	Write clearly, thoroughly and succinctly in accessible language?	0 1 2 3 4 5 6 7 8 9 10 Comments
11.	Challenge poor practice when you see it, from other agencies such as children's social care, health, etc.	0 1 2 3 4 5 6 7 8 9 10 Comments
12.	Achieve improved outcomes for children through your involvement and your influence on parental understanding/ behaviour and/or professional practice	0 1 2 3 4 5 6 7 8 9 10 Comments
13.	Give yourself an overall score based on the average of the scores you have given for the questions above.	0 1 2 3 4 5 6 7 8 9 10 Comments
14.	Based on your scores identify up to three things that you wish to do to strengthen your practice. This may need to involve other people through training/ supervision/mentoring, etc.	1. 2. 3.

Activity 5: Peer review of assessments

Aim

To encourage peer mentoring and practice sharing in the team in relation to analysis.

> ## Objectives
>
> By the end of the activity participants will have:
>
> - given constructive feedback to each other about the quality of analysis in assessments
> - shared experience and expertise across the team
> - reflected on peer review of assessments.

Time

1½ hours, plus preparation of 3–4 hours.

Ideal numbers

6–12 (need an even number).

Method

- In advance of the session, ask each practitioner to identify and provide you with an assessment they have completed that is fairly typical of their practice. To make the selection more random, suggest that each practitioner uses his or her last assessment.

- Use a code to mark which assessment belongs to which participant as this will prove useful later on.

- Attach a feedback sheet (page 147) to the back of each assessment.

- Also in advance of the session, read each assessment and make a note of its strengths and weaknesses, particularly in relation to analysis, using the trigger questions on the feedback sheet.

- Invite participants to form pairs.

- Distribute two assessments to each pair, using the codes to make sure that no one is looking at their own.

- Invite participants to read through each assessment and note the strengths and areas for improvement on the attached feedback sheet, using the trigger questions as prompts. Tell the pairs of participants that they will have at least 20–30 minutes to discuss and comment on each assessment.

- After 20–30 minutes, collect the assessments and then use the codes to help you redistribute them to their authors.

- Tell participants that they now have 15 minutes to read the comments written on their assessment.

- After 15 minutes, encourage the participants, still in their pairs, to discuss their response to the comments.

- Reconvene the group and invite feedback from everyone, as individuals. Prompt with questions such as: Was it helpful to have this feedback? Did it ring true or were you surprised by the comments? Is there anything you would like to ask, for clarification? How has it left you feeling? Are there any actions you will take as a result?

Facilitator's notes

It is important that all assessments provided are of the same type, that is they should all be initial or all core assessments. This exercise can work for both types but core assessments will take more time. Using core assessments may provide opportunities for a more in-depth examination and reflection.

In some teams it would be possible to encourage direct discussion between those writing the comments and those in receipt. The notes that you, as facilitator, made (concerning strengths and areas for improvement) can also be offered as part of the discussion. There is a risk of participants feeling exposed or becoming defensive. Judgement will need to be used to decide how far to take the discussion and whether it is likely to be helpful and productive for the individual participants and the team as a whole.

Feedback sheet

Trigger questions

Is the assessment needs-led?

Have parents and children and other professionals been appropriately involved?

Is there evidence of differing hypotheses being considered and tested out?

Is there evidence of any analysis of the facts or weighing up of options?

Is there any evidence of research or theory being used to support arguments?

Do actions flow logically from the information gathered and its analysis?

Have decisions been discussed with children and carers?

Strengths	Areas for improvement

Activity 6: Miracle question exercise

Aim

To encourage team members to be imaginative in describing their aspirations for children and for practice in their team.

Objectives

By the end of the activity participants will have:

- drawn from solution-focused work and 'thought outside the box' to imagine what practice in the team could be like

- created a series of tangible aspirational statements about the way in which practice could develop in the team and agency

- created an action plan to work towards these aspirational statements.

Time

From 1–3 hours depending on how far the exercise is taken.

Ideal numbers

Any number.

Method

- Ask participants to close their eyes and relax. Explain that they are going to be taken on a guided fantasy.

- Read out the following paragraph slowly, pausing to allow people time to think at the relevant points.

  Imagine that when you go to sleep tonight, a miracle occurs and three years pass. During that time, everything has changed and assessment practice has improved in your team and agency; so now analysis is an integral part of assessments; decisions and actions flowing from assessment are needs led, completely appropriate and most likely to lead to the best outcomes for children and their families; and there are opportunities for reflection and team learning.

- Tell participants that they will be asked a number of questions; and that they will be given about 30 seconds to answer each. Stress that they will not be sharing their answers yet.

- Ask the following questions, allowing 30 seconds between each one for participants to think about their responses.

  - When you wake up and go into work what will you immediately notice has changed?
  - How will you personally be behaving?
  - How will practitioners and managers be behaving?
  - How will the atmosphere in the team have changed?

148

- How will children and parents be behaving?
- Will there be other visual evidence of changes?
- How will other professionals be behaving?

■ If participants have closed their eyes, ask them to open them now.

■ Repeat the first question and invite participants to shout out the thoughts they had in response to it. Record all responses on a flip chart – even if they are light-hearted.

■ Do the same for each of the subsequent questions (that is, repeat the question and record the shouted out answers).

■ Examine the lists that have been made and ask participants to reflect on how far the current situation in their workplace is from the idealised picture.

■ Ask the team to try and prioritise three or four areas in which they could work towards achieving change. If it is a large team, divide it up into two or three smaller groups, then ask each group to identify three priority areas; and then reconvene the whole group to debate and agree the top three to five priorities.

■ Once the priorities are agreed, ask the team to develop an action plan to achieve these; for example, by answering key questions concerning what/when/who uses the action planning template (page 138). Stress the importance of ascribing tasks to named people and agreeing a timescale. Record the action plan and agree a date on which to review progress.

Facilitator's notes

This exercise does require that participants leave behind their everyday constraints and be imaginative, so some judgement will have to be exercised as to how ready a team or group are to do this. If they are feeling stressed or bogged down, this type of activity might feel a bit too esoteric. On the other hand, it could be a welcome relief. There is room for some humour here and people will make some 'off the wall' suggestions but try to take everything on board and facilitate the team in prioritising actions that are likely to bear some fruit and be most useful to the team's development.

Activity 7: Story telling exercise

Aim

To highlight the importance of accuracy and context when sharing information about people's personal lives, and to encourage empathy for those about whom information is shared.

Time

30 to 40 minutes.

Ideal numbers

Large group, e.g. 12, 16, 20 – divisible by four for groups to be formed.

Method

This activity requires a sufficient number of participants for them to form one or more groups of four.

- Ask each set of four participants to sit in two pairs. Name them **A** and **B** (side-by-side) and the facing pair **C** and **D**, as shown below.

  participant **A**   participant **B**

  participant **C**   participant **D**

- Invite each participant to think of an experience they have had (that they are willing to share, i.e. not too emotive) that was either very scary or very exciting.

- Tell the participants that they will tell their story, in the order you instruct them to, and that they will have three minutes to do so.

- For each group of four, invite participant **A** to tell **C** (who they should be facing) their story. At the same time, invite **B** to tell **D** their story. Stop them after three minutes.

- Now ask **C** to tell **A** their story and **D** to tell **B** theirs. Once again, give them three minutes.

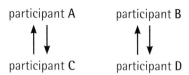

- Ask all the participants to turn their chairs round so that **A** now faces **B**, and **C** now faces **D**.

- Invite **A** to tell **B** the story they just heard from **C**; and invite **C** to tell **D** the story they just heard from **A**. Stop them after three minutes.

- Invite the participants to swap over again, so that **B** can tell **A** the story they heard from **D**; and **D** can tell **C** the story they heard from **B**.

participant A $\rightleftarrows$ participant B

participant C $\rightleftarrows$ participant D

- Tell **B** and **D** to swap seats.

- Invite **A** to tell **D** the story they have just heard, which will be **D**'s story being repeated back to them. Likewise, invite **B** to tell **C** the story they have just heard. This should mean everyone at this stage gets three minutes to hear their own story told back to them. Invite the participants to swap over again so that **C** and **D** have an opportunity to repeat **A** and **B**'s original story to them.

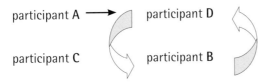

participant A ⟶ participant D

participant C   participant B

- Invite participants to quietly reflect on what it was like to have their story told back to them.

- Ask them, for example: Was it accurate or distorted? Were there key details missing? How did they feel about knowing their story was being told to another when they couldn't listen to what was said? Encourage the participants to draw parallels with the experiences of service users giving us information; but stress how diluted and artificial this demonstration is in comparison.

6. Challenges and opportunities for analytical practice

This chapter discusses further some of the lessons to be drawn from the literature and the Putting analysis into assessment project regarding what helps and hinders analytical and reflective practice.

It goes on to consider the particular challenges that arise in multi-agency working and some of the things that can be done to reduce bias and distorted thinking.

It then makes suggestions as to what can be done at the team, supervisory and organisational level to create and sustain a practice culture that supports continuous learning and reflective practice. In particular, it considers how evidence-based practice can be promoted at every level within an organisation to turn the rhetoric into reality.

Lessons from the project

There were some general points made by participants during the Putting analysis into assessment project that it seems useful to consider here. The teams involved were drawn from two settings – which contrasted geographically, demographically and in terms of resources and challenges facing them – but the overall lessons learned from both areas were broadly similar. In both areas, feedback indicated that there were some important gains for the teams from being involved in the project, which went some way to improving the analytical practice within the teams. These were: getting analysis firmly on their agenda; a heightened awareness of the pitfalls of using intuitive methods alone; and more focused attention on analytical approaches.

The introduction of theoretical notions about how to think critically and the passing on of the 'tools' included within this toolkit was, in the most part, received positively and has added to the practical resources available to team members. Significantly, the time and space that sessions allowed was as important as the use of the tools themselves. The practice development sessions where, instead of introducing tools and approaches, there was time to think about analysis (through case discussions, looking at each other's reports, examining conclusions and understanding decisions), were undoubtedly as useful to practitioners. It seemed that putting aside time for the practice development sessions in the presence of (or at least with the encouragement of) team managers, provided a much-needed opportunity for individual and team reflection. Furthermore, participants reported that once analysis was firmly on their team agendas there was more focus on it within supervision and in peer discussions.

The importance of reflection time as an essential prerequisite for undertaking good quality analysis within assessments arose time and again.

It is perhaps not surprising that resource issues, which impact on the time available to practitioners for reflection, pose one of the greatest challenges to analytical practice. In many agencies, limited resources lead to high volumes of work that, despite all intentions to the contrary, result in reactive practice. Additionally, many practitioners and some managers on the project highlighted that their ability to be needs-led in assessments was influenced significantly by an awareness of service constraints.

However, much can be done at an organisational level to enable practitioners to undertake assessments that thoroughly identify needs, both in order to help the agency meet them and to identify where they cannot do so. Some practitioners on the project told us of a tendency to see fixed timescales and deadlines for reports as dates by which they had to have finished assessments, even when they had established only a partial picture of the family's circumstances. This highlighted the importance of agencies supporting practitioners by encouraging them to acknowledge in reports 'how far they've got' in their assessments, in order that they do not feel under pressure to say more than they know.

The physical working environment also plays an important part, whilst open-plan offices can be conducive to receiving on-the-spot peer support they are also generally noisy. It is important that workers at all levels have opportunities to work in quiet rooms at times when they particularly need to focus on a specific piece of work or grapple with the meaning of lots of information to help them consider their analysis.

The ability of practitioners to draw critically on research findings and theory clearly plays an important part in efforts to improve analysis within the social work task. However, when we asked practitioners on the project and in training courses about their perceived levels of competence and confidence in drawing on research evidence and theory, they frequently responded that they did not have time available to them for reading, although nearly all of them wanted to be more aware of up-to-date research. Individual practitioners clearly had varying levels of confidence and competence; and levels of experience had an impact on this. Newly qualified practitioners often have up-to-date knowledge but need to build up their confidence in applying it in practice, whereas those who had been qualified for some time can think that their knowledge levels have lapsed. It is often the case with learning and experience that the more we learn the more we realise we need to learn. Another cause cited for low confidence levels was the frequent criticism of social workers through negative media portrayal and what some practitioners perceived as low expectations among professionals and families about their profession.

Social workers also often expressed the view that they were not seen as experts in the court arena and were reluctant to portray themselves as such. Some were reluctant to cite research evidence or to link their analysis to theory in their assessment reports because they did not think they had sufficient grasp of research to respond to the challenge they might meet in court. They expected that if other 'experts' were brought in to erode their arguments they might be 'setting themselves up' by using research and, in turn, all their reasoning would be called into question. This is an understandable concern and is compounded further if legal advisors and agencies are not clear with staff about what is expected of them with regard to using research evidence within reports. For this reason Research in Practice are undertaking a Change project called *Social work and the use of research evidence in relation to children's cases in the family court*, to examine and make recommendations in this difficult area.

Some of the factors that the project teams thought supported analytical practice were offered as follows.

- 'Supportive' team culture

- Constructive debate being encouraged within the team

- Good supervision [one team particularly noted the usefulness of having a manager who asks for their views before giving her own and who then challenges constructively]

- There was no such thing as a 'stupid question' [said one team]; and there is a 'safe atmosphere' for team members to learn and question things [said another]

- Joint work, particularly in complex and long-term cases, helps too; a second opinion from colleagues helps us [workers] keep sight of standards of care and 'thresholds' as family situations can become 'normalised' in the minds of workers through exposure to a family over time

- Drawing on theory and research findings

- Commitment by managers to professional development

- Ethnically and gender diverse teams reflective of local population

- Experienced team members

- Team study days

- External inter-agency forums.

It is clear that whilst social workers can do many things, including using tools such as those in this toolkit, to enhance their own practice, the systems they work within also need to support them in the task. What can be done at the organisational level to improve analytical practice is discussed below (under 'Creating and sustaining an environment for continuous practice development) but first, consideration needs to be given to the specific issues that arise in inter-agency working.

Reflection and analysis in multi-agency contexts

As discussed in the section on Preparing oneself in Chapter 2, page 9, any decisions that a practitioner makes are influenced by their emotions, values, reasoning skills, practice wisdom and formal knowledge. It is important (but not easy) for the practitioner to try and identify these influences in order to be transparent in their decisions, but even more so when there are a range of professionals involved with a decision. As well as each individual being encouraged to be reflective about their own personal and professional responses (as in reality these are rarely absolutely separable), they need to find ways to encourage agencies to bring an awareness of what norms and practices they bring to an assessment because of the context in which they work. Examples of such norms may be: thresholds, knowledge of resource availability and past experience of how their agency has worked in similar circumstances.

Whilst groups have the advantage of many heads instead of one, they also bring with them the potential for bias and distorted thinking – or 'Groupthink' as Janis (1982) called it – which are often caused by power issues and the avoidance of conflict. Munro (2002) summarised what Janis identified as the following tendencies when groups think together: an overestimation of the group; closed mindedness; and pressure to conform. Munro also summarised the following suggested measures designed to help to protect against groupthink.

1. Group leaders should explicitly encourage dissent and criticism including of their own position.

2. Group leaders should let the lowest ranking members of the group speak first and should themselves refrain from stating their personal preferences at the outset.

3. Groups should set up other groups with other leaders to consider the same question, allowing for a comparison of responses.

4. Group members should periodically discuss the group's deliberations with trusted associates and give feedback on these discussions to the group.

5. Groups should invite outside experts or qualified colleagues to attend the group meetings and should encourage them to challenge the group consensus.

6. Groups should appoint one member to be the official 'devil's advocate', to disagree with the consensus.

The consequences of distorted decisions have such a significant impact on service users that it is important to take active measures to guard against distorted group thinking, whether or not service users are present during group deliberations.

Creating and sustaining an environment for continuous practice development

For effective analytical practice to be the norm – that is the baseline that it should be for service delivery – the teams and agencies in which they operate should support and encourage good analytical thinking and practice at every level. This involves creating and sustaining an agency culture that supports continuous development and reflection, both organisationally and on a practitioner and team level. This section will consider what can be done at the team and team manager level and at the organisational level to create a practice culture that supports analysis.

Agency culture

The leadership role is vital in encouraging critical thinking and reflection; and in giving permission for people to carve out the time they need to do so properly. The tone set within the agency in its priorities and approach to practice will permeate throughout the whole service, so it is important to deliberately cultivate the characteristics of agency culture covered in this section.

It is not enough for managers to talk about evidence-informed practice. Leaders of organisations and in turn their managers and staff need the 'raw materials' – including time and a valuing of 'thinking space' – to utilise evidence from a range of sources meaningfully. Workers should be encouraged to draw on theory and research, which involves providing them with the resources to do so easily and efficiently. Enabling evidence-based practice specifically is discussed in more detail later in this section.

Agencies also need to factor in and facilitate time for direct work with children, as a failure to adequately explore children's needs and experiences is often one of the most significant flaws in assessments.

An increased tendency towards 'managerialism' with components of practice measured and checked in mechanical ways can, if its limitations are not acknowledged, erode professionalism and autonomy and be insensitive at the case level. For example, an agency can place a high priority on fulfilling a Performance indicator relating to Looked after Children reviews going ahead on time, but lose sight of the importance of enabling young people to participate in the review by implementing local rules – such as 'all review meetings must go ahead' even if the social worker is off sick, or the parent or child is sick – that can lead to a meeting that is of less value than it could have been.

There is clearly a need to collate information regarding whether standards are met, but efforts need to be made to ensure that practitioners do not think this is of a higher priority than service users' needs. It is more helpful to concentrate on how much time the worker spends with the child; in what range of settings; and what sense they have been able to make of what the child is communicating or experiencing; and to assist practitioners to achieve the analysis of information confidently and meaningfully.

The importance that senior managers appear to place on reflective practice should be demonstrated through their own actions and ways of doing things. For example, if leaders demonstrate open-mindedness; recognition that they can make mistakes and can always learn from them; and that getting at the truth is more important than winning an argument; then they are better placed to encourage this ethos throughout the whole organisation. If the agency culture is to expect workers to be decisive and strong in sticking to 'right' opinions once formed, it can be very difficult for workers to go back on their own thinking or be self-critical or to revise their conclusions – even though to be open to doing so is good practice. As Munro (2002, p.145) puts it, it can be tempting to 'close one's eyes and be uncritical'.

Finally, attention to analytic methods at the agency level helps guard against practice that is oppressive or unwittingly discriminating. The more explicit and clear we can be in our thinking, the more we can empower and involve service users.

Supervision

Perhaps one of the most direct influences on the ability of practitioners to work to optimum effectiveness is the quality of supervision available to them.

It is clear that both intuitive and analytical approaches have strengths and weaknesses. It was shown in Preparing for assessments (page 10) how a skilled practitioner will, at any one time, be drawing on a range of skills and methods along the continuum of intuition and analysis. It is therefore crucial that, in supervision, skills in intuition and empathy are nurtured and valued, while more objective mechanisms to aid analytical thinking are also encouraged.

Supervisors should prioritise the need for an overview or chronology, not as a paper exercise or because a court process requires it, but in order to provide rich information that may help a practitioner grow nearer to understanding how problems for a family came to be over time.

Supervisors can also support analysis by ensuring that a range of explanations for causes of concerns are explored over time, and by encouraging practitioners to seek to disconfirm their original hypotheses, actively hypothesising as described in Chapter 2 (page 23).

Practitioners should be enabled or challenged by supervisors to avoid being steered too readily into what can become a fairly entrenched 'agency view' in relation to families over time. This is particularly important with cases that have been known about over long periods of time. New workers to a case are often given an overview based on longstanding judgements. In particular if they lack confidence, experience or feel disempowered by the hierarchy, it is far easier to go along with this than to look anew at the family or child's circumstances and to challenge it. Tools such as the Critical Decision method (page 125) can be helpful to supervisors when assisting practitioners to learn from their own practice, as it uses a process that challenges the practitioner to really reflect on what they did and why. Klein (2000, p 104) says experts learn and derive insights through accurate, diagnostic and timely feedback; and through reviewing past experiences. Supervisors are often well placed to provide such feedback.

What can teams do?

If an analytical approach to assessment work is to be embedded in a team's ethos and work, it is important that it is owned and responsibility is shared by all team members.

Teams should ensure that, as a group, they are fully aware of what existing structures and resources are in place to support them in their practice and development. These include local training, inter-agency forums, and PQ training opportunities; and organisations providing practitioners with opportunities to access information and web-based publications. Also, the use of existing tools such as the Questionnaires and Scales that accompany the *Framework for Assessment of Children in Need and their Families* (DH and others 2000) could be encouraged, if not already being utilised.

Many teams use their meeting time to go beyond the business of the team's day-to-day functions to spending time reflecting, learning or considering practice. Some of the tools in this toolkit could be used to focus that time on practice development sessions. With the many pressures social workers face, they might feel some resistance to the introduction of more formal analytic tools and to moving away from intuitive practice, particularly where 'tools' mean more forms to fill in. This is more likely if intuition and analysis are presented as polarised approaches in a way that fails to acknowledge the essential skills in empathy and intuition, without which practice would be ineffective and robotic.

If information officers are available to the team then they could seek out research evidence or literature reviews for practitioners on a given subject to assist their thinking in particular cases. However, where there is no such post, teams can support themselves by allocating designated areas of knowledge responsibility, to individual team members, for example someone signs up to specialist forums regarding domestic violence, someone else for asylum seeker issues and they then share their learning during team meetings, providing handouts or pointers to more detailed information where appropriate.

Developing a more evidence-based approach to practice at an organisational level

> *Evidence-based decision-making requires not only a sound knowledge base regarding abuse and neglect but also an understanding of how the process of assessment can be undermined, and that steps that can be taken to protect against this.*

> *(Geraldine Macdonald, 2001 p.249)*

As stated throughout this toolkit, improving the participant's analytic capacity involves actively trying to counter the natural tendencies for bias that undermine their practice, such as becoming attached to their early conclusions about families. As well as suggesting ways to identify when this is happening and tools to assist practitioners in their analysis of children's needs (as provided in this book), drawing on up-to-date research evidence is also an important part of enhancing the quality of assessments.

However, many practitioners are less clear than they would like to be about the content of research evidence, or how to access the information that will be most directly useful in their practice. To assist with this, we have provided a few examples of useful websites in the section Resources and useful information.

The sorts of 'evidence' referred to here are national and local research findings; good practice models; findings of service evaluations, including service-user feedback and data on short- and long-term outcomes for service users; inspection reports; and summaries of inspections.

If organisations are to truly promote and support evidence-based practice they need to consider drawing up a strategy to do so, appointing a steering group or lead person to oversee its implementation; and to draw up concrete action plans to bring about change.

Evidence-based practice should be a regular agenda item in meetings at every level and research evidence should be referred to in policy documents, and strategic plans.

User feedback should be sought, analysed and shared with staff along with any information that is available on short- and long-term outcomes for service users.

Resources such as specialist library access and information officers who can help others to find and make sense of information should be considered. Also, practitioners need easy access to the internet from or near their desks. Journals and books should be made readily available and learning from conferences and research events should be disseminated effectively within the organisation. Similar mechanisms for dissemination could be employed on a team level; with PQ students for example being given opportunities to share their learning with colleagues.

Supervision policies should stress that supporting evidence-based practice is a function of supervision. Development plans and appraisals of practitioners should pay attention to their needs in building on their practice in this area.

Finally, and perhaps the hardest to achieve, is that time for reflection and reading should be factored in when considering what individual practitioners and teams can achieve in terms of outputs.

References

Adcock, M (2000) 'The core assessment process: How to synthesise information and make judgements', in Horwath, J (ed) *The Child's World: Assessing children in need. The reader.* London: NSPCC.

Advisory Council on the Misuse of Drugs (2003) *Hidden Harm: Responding to the needs of children of problem drug users – The report of an inquiry by the Advisory Council on the misuse of drugs.* HMSO.

Anderson, T (1990) *The Reflecting Team: Dialogues and Metadialogues.* Broadstairs: Borgmann.

Barlow, J and Scott, J (2010) *Safeguarding in the 21st Century: Where to now.* Dartington: Research in Practice.

Barnes, V and Chand, A (2001) 'Initial Assessments in Child Protection: The reality of practice', *Practice* 12, 4, 5–16.

Barratt, M and Hodson, R (2006) *Firm Foundations: A practical guide to organsiational support for the use of research evidence.* Dartington: Research in Practice.

Bell, M, Shaw, I, Sinclair, I (2007) *The Integrated Children's System: An evaluation of the practice process and consequences of ICS in councils with a social services responsibility.* York: University of York.

Bennett, F and White, J (2004) *Consulting Children Under Fourteen on Their Views of People Who Help Them in Times of Difficulty.* Edinburgh: NHS Education for Scotland.

Brandon, M, Bailey, S, Belderson, P, Gardner, R, Sidebotham, P, Dodsworth, J, Warren, C and Black, J. (2009) *Understanding Serious Case Reviews and their Impact: A biennial analysis of serious case reviews 2005–07.* Research Report DCSF-RR129. Norwich: University of East Anglia.

Brandon, M, Belderson, P, Warren, C, Howe, D, Gardner, R, Dodsworth, J and Black, J (2008) *Analysing Child Deaths and Serious Injury through Abuse and Neglect: What can we learn? A biennial analysis of serious case reviews 2003-2005.* Research Report DCSF-RR023. Norwich: University of East Anglia.

Broad, B (2004) 'Kinship care for children in the UK: Messages from research, lessons for policy and practice', *European Journal of Social Work*, 7, 2, 211–28.

Broad, B, Hayes, R, and Rushforth, C (2001) *Kinship Care for Vulnerable Young People.* York: Joseph Rowntree Foundation.

Bronfenbrenner, U (1989) 'Ecological systems theory' *Annals of Child Development*, 6, 187–249.

Brophy, J (2006) *Research Review: Child Care Proceedings under the Children Act 1989.* Department for Constitutional Affairs, DCA Research Series 5/06. Oxford Centre for Family Law and Policy, University of Oxford. Butler, I and Williamson, H (1994) *Children Speak: Children, trauma and social work.* Harlow: Longman.

C4EO (2010) *The views and experiences of children and young people who have been through the child protection/safeguarding system. Review of literature and Consultation Report.* London: C4EO Calder, Martin C and Hackett, S (eds) (2003) *Assessment in Childcare: Using and developing frameworks for practice.* Russell House Publishing.

Calder, Martin C, Harold, Gordon TMD and Howarth, Emma L (2004) *Children Living with Domestic Violence: Towards a framework for assessment.* Russell House.

Carvel, J (2004) *Britain violates rights of child says U.N. Committee on the rights of the child.* Guardian online 29.11.2004.

Cash, S (2001) 'Risk assessment in child welfare: The art and science', *Children and Youth Services Review*, 23, 11, 811–30.

Cawson, P (2002) *Child Maltreatment in the family. The experience of a national sample of young people.* London NSPCC.

Caxton, G (1999) *Wise Up: The challenge of lifelong learning.* London: Bloomsbury.

Children's Rights Alliance for England (2008) *Listen and Change: A Guide to Children and Young People's Participation Rights.* London: Participation Works.

Cleaver, H, Unel, I and Aldgate, A (1999) *Children's Needs – Parenting Capacity: The impact of parental mental illness, problem alcohol and drug use and domestic violence on children's development.* London: The Stationery Office.

Cleaver, H and Nicholson, D (2007) *Parental Learning Disability and Children's Needs.* London: Jessica Kingsley Publishers.

Cleaver, H, Nicholson, D, Tarr, S and Cleaver, D (2007) *Child Protection, Domestic Violence and Parental Substance Misuse: Family Experiences and Effective Practice.* London: Jessica Kingsley Publishers.

Cleaver, H and Walker, S (2004a) *Assessing Children's Needs and Circumstances: The impact of the Assessment Framework.* London: Jessica Kingsley.

Cleaver, H, Walker, S and Meadows, P (2004) *Assessing Children's Needs and Circumstances: The Impact of the Assessment Framework.* London: Jessica Kingsley Publishers.

Cleaver, H and Walker, S (2004b) 'From policy to practice: The implementation of a new framework for social work assessments of children and families', *Child and Family Social Work*, 9, 81–90.

Daniel, B, Taylor, J, Scott, J and Barbour, M (2009) *Noticing and Helping the Neglected Child: A Systematic Review of the Literature.* Unpublished Report. London: Department for Children, Schools and Families.

Daniel, B, Wassell, S, and Gilligan, R (2010) *Child Development for Child Care and Protection Workers.* London: Jessica Kingsley.

Davies, C and Ward H (2011) *Safeguarding Children Across Services: Messages from research on identifying and responding to child maltreatment.* London: DFE.

Department for Children Schools and Families (2010) *Integrated Children's System Guidance: Analysing and recording significant harm.* London: HMSO.

Department for Education (2011) *A child-centred system: The Government's response to the Munro review of child protection.* London DfE.

Department of Health (1988) *Protecting Children: A Guide for Social Workers Undertaking a Comprehensive Assessment.* London: HMSO.

Department of Health (1995) *Child Protection: Messages from research.*

Department of Health (2002) *Safeguarding Children: The joint chief inspectors report on arrangements to safeguard children.* London: Department of Health.

Department of Health (2003) 12th Annual Report of the Chief Inspector of Social Services. London: HMSO.

Department of Health and others (2000) *Framework for the Assessment of Children in Need and their Families: The family pack of questionnaires and scales.* London: The Stationery Office.

Department of Health, Cox, A and Bentovim, A (2000) *The Family Assessment Pack of Questionnaires and Scales.* London: The Stationery Office. Donnelly, RR (2010) *Practice Guide: Chronologies.* Social Work Inspection Agency for Scotland.

Dreyfus, H and Dreyfus, S (1986) *Mind over Machine: The power of human intuition on expertise in the era of the computer.* New York: The Free Press.

Farmer, E and Lutman, E (2010) *Case Management and Outcomes for Neglected Children Returned to their Parents: A five year follow-up study. Report to the Department for Children, Schools and Families.* Bristol: School for Policy Studies, University of Bristol.

Farmer, E and Owen, M (1995) *Child Protection Practice: Private risks and public remedies.* HMSO.

Farmer, E, Sturgess, W and O'Neill, T (2008) *The Reunification of Looked After Children With Their Parents: Patterns interventions and outcomes. Report to the Department for Children, Schools and Families.* Bristol: School for Policy Studies, University of Bristol.

Fauth, R, Jelicic, H, Hart, D, Burton, S, Shemmings, D and others (2010) *Effective Practice to protect children Living in Highly Resistant Families.* London: C4EO.

Featherstone, B and Evans, H (2004) *Children experiencing maltreatment: who do they turn to?* London: NSPCC.

Forrester, D (2004) 'Social work assessments with parents who misuse drugs or alcohol' in Phillips, R *Children Exposed to Parental Substance Misuse: Implications for Family Placement* London: BAAF.

Forrester, D and Harwin, J (2008) 'Parental substance misuse and child welfare: outcomes for children two years after referral', *British Journal of Social Work*, 38: 1518–1535.

Garmezy, N (1973) 'Competence and adaptation of adult schizophrenic patients and children at risk' in Dea, SR (ed) *Schizophrenia: The first ten Dean Award Lectures.* New York: MSS information Corporation.

Garmezy, N and Streitman, S (1974) 'Children at risk: The search for the antecedents of schizophrenia. Part 1. Conceptual models and research methods', *Schizophrenia Bulletin* 8 (8): 14–90.

Garvey, B, Madden, M, Violi, C, Vitali, C, Spigelman, A and Tracey, G (2008) *How do young adults seek help?* London: Vodafone Foundation and NFP Synergy.

Gilligan, R (2001) *Promoting resilience: a resource guide on working with children in the care system.* London: BAAF.

Gilligan, R (2009) *Promoting Resilience: Supporting children and young people who are in care, adopted or in need.* London: BAAF.

Gopfert, M, Webster, J and Seeman, M (eds) (2004) *Parental psychiatric disorder: distressed parents and their families.* Cambridge: Cambridge University Press.

Grotberg, E (1995) *A Guide to Promoting Resilience in Children: Strengthening the human spirit.* The Hague: Bernard van Leer Foundation.

Hammond, R (1996) *Human Judgement and Social Policy*, Oxford University Press, cited in O'Sullivan, T (1999) Decision-making in Social Work. Palgrave.

Haringey Local Safeguarding Children Board (2010) Second serious case overview report relating to Peter Connelly. London: DfE.

Hart, D 'Assessment prior to birth', Ch. 15, in Horwath, J (ed)(2001) *The Child's World: Assessing children in need.* London: Jessica Kingsley.

Hart, D and Powell, J (2006) *Adult Drug Problems, Children's Needs: Assessing the impact of parental drug use – A toolkit for practitioners.* London: National Children's Bureau.

Harvey Jones, J quote from http://www.continuitycentral.com/quotes,alphabetical.pdf (accessed 26 August 2011).

Helm, D (2010) *Making sense of child and family assessment: understanding children's needs.* London: Jessica Kingsley.

Higgins, DJ and McCabe, MP (2000) 'Multi-type maltreatment and long-term adjustment of adults', *Child Abuse Review*, 9, 6-18.

HM Government (2006) Common Assessment Framework guides. London: HM Government. *http:www. everychildmatters.gov.uk/resources-and-practice/G00063*

Holland, S (2004) *Child and Family Assessment in Social Work Practice.* London: Sage Publications.

Holland, S. (2010) *Child and Family Assessment in Social Work Practice* (2nd Edition). London: Sage Publications.

Hollows, A 'Making professional judgements in the framework for the assessment of children in need and their families, Ch. 3, in Calder, Martin C and Hackett, S (eds) (2003) *Assessment in Childcare: Using and developing frameworks for practice.* Russell House Publishing.

Horwath, J (ed) (2001) *The Child's World: Assessing children in need.* London: Jessica Kingsley.

Humphreys, C, Houghton ,C and Ellis, J (2008) *Better outcomes for children and young people experiencing domestic abuse: directions for good practice.* Scottish Government.

Janis, I (1982) 'Groupthink: Psychological studies of policy decisions and fiascos', Boston, MA: Houghton Mifflin, cited in Munro, E (2002) *Effective Child Protection.* Sage Publications.

Jones, D (2006) 'Communicating with children about adverse experiences', in Aldgate, J, Rose, W and Jeffery, C (2006) *The developing world of the child.* London: Jessica Kingsley Publishers.

Jones, D (2009) 'Assessment of parenting', in Horwath, J (ed.) (2009) *The Child's World: The comprehensive guide to assessing children in need.* 2nd ed. London: Jessica Kingsley Publishers.

Jones, D, Hindley, P and Ramchandi, A (2006) 'Making plans, assessment, intervention and evaluating outcomes', in Aldgate, J and others (eds) *The Developing World of the Child.* London: Jessica Kingsley.

Keene, NH (1999) *Education by Design – Coaching kit Level 2,* The Critical Skills Program. Antioch: Antioch University.

Kerr, S quote from http://www.continuitycentral.com/quotes,alphabetical.pdf (accessed 26 August 2011).

Klein, G (2000) *Sources of Power: How people make decisions.* Cambridge MA: MIT Press.

Laming, HW (2003) *The Victoria Climbie Inquiry: Report of an Inquiry by Lord Laming.* Norwich: HMSO.

Lombard, D (2009) '*Report slams placement of teenager who abused children: Vale of Glamorgan Council social services director apologises for 'fundamental flaws',* Community Care online, 18 May 2009.

Luthar, SS (ed.) (2003) *Resilience and Vulnerability: Adaptation in the context of childhood adversities.* Cambridge: Cambridge University Press.

Mainey, A, Ellis, A and Lewis, J (2009) *Children's Views of Services: A rapid review.* London: National Children's Bureau.

Mariathasan, J (2009) *Children talking to childline about sexual abuse.* London: NSPCC Childline casenotes.

Masten, AS (1989) 'Resilience in Development: Implications of the study of successful adaptation for developmental psychopathology', in Cicchetti, D (ed.) *The Emergence of a Discipline: Rochester symposium on developmental psychopathology* (Vol. 1, pp. 261–294). Hillsdale, NJ: Erlbaum.

Masten, AS Best, KM and Garmezy, N (1990) 'Resilience and development: Contributions from the study of children who overcome adversity', *Development and Psychopathology 2* (04): 425–44.

MacDonald, G (2001) *Effective Interventions for Child Abuse and Neglect: An evidence-based approach to planning and evaluating interventions.* Chichester: Wiley.

McCracken, DG (1988) *The Long Interview.* Beverly Hills, CA: Sage.

Miller, WR and Rollnick, S (2002) *Motivational Interviewing: Preparing people for change* 2nd ed. London: The Guilford Press.

Moon, J (1999) *Learning Journals: A handbook for academics, students and professional development.* London: Kogan Page.

Morgan, R (2005) *Getting the Best from Complaints: The children's view – what children and young people think about the government's proposals to change the social services complaints procedure.* Newcastle: Office of the Children's Rights Director.

Morgan, R (2011) *Younger Children's Views: A report of children's views by the Children's Rights Director for England.* Manchester: Ofsted.

Munro, E (1999) 'Common errors of reasoning in child protection work', *Child Abuse & Neglect*, 23, 8, 745–58.

Munro, E (2002) *Effective Child Protection.* Sage Publications.

Munro, E (2008) *Effective Child Protection.* 2nd ed. London: Sage Publications.

Munro, E (2011) *The Munro Review of Child Protection: Final Report – A child-centred system.* Norwich: HMSO.

Nelson, S (ed) (2008) *See Us Hear Us: Schools working with sexually abused young people.* Dundee: Violence is Preventable..

Newman, T and Blackburn, S (2002) *Transitions in the Lives of Children and Young People: Resilience Factors.* Edinburgh: Scottish Executive.

NSPCC (1997) *Turning Points: A resource pack for communicating with children* (Module 2, Foundation Part of pack). NSPCC.

Office of the Children's Rights Director for England (2011) *Messages for Munro.* A report of children's views collected for Prof Eileen Munro by children's rights director of England Office for standards in education, children's services and skills.

Ofsted (2008) *Learning Lessons, Taking Action: Ofsted's evaluations of serious case reviews 1 April 2007 to 31 March 2008.* London: Oftsed.

Olsen, R and Wates, M (2003) *Disabled Parents: Examining research assumptions.* Dartington: Research in Practice.

O'Sullivan, T (1999) *Decision-making in Social Work.* Basingstoke: Palgrave.

Phillips, R (ed) (2004) *Children Exposed to Parental Substance Misuse Implications for Family Placement.* BAAF.

Prior, V, Lynch, M, Glaser, D (1994) 'Responding to child sexual abuse: an evaluation of social work by children and their carers', *Child and Family Social Work*, 4(2), May 1999, pp.131-143.

Prochaska, JO, Norcross, JC and Diclemente, CC (1994) *Changing for Good: The revolutionary program that explains the six stages of change and teaches you how to free yourself from bad habits.* New York: William Morrow & Co.

Reder, P and Duncan, S (1999) *Lost Innocents: A follow-up study of fatal child abuse.* Routledge.

Rutter, M (1993) 'Resilience some conceptual considerations', *Journal of Adolescent Health*, 14, 626–31.

Sawyer, E (2009) *Building Resilience in Families Under Stress: Supporting families affected by parental substance misuse and/or mental health problems.* London: National Children's Bureau.

Schön, D A (1983) *The Reflective Practitioner: How professionals think in action.* New York: Basic Books.

Scott, D (1998) 'A qualitative study of social work assessment in cases of alleged child abuse', *British Journal of Social Work*, 28 (1): 73–88.

Seden, J, Sinclair, R, Robbins, D, and Pont, C (2001) *Studies Informing the Framework for the Assessment of Children in Need and their Families.* The Stationery Office.

Shaw, I (1997) *Be your Own Evaluator.* Wrexham: Prospects.

Sheldon, B (1987) 'The psychology of incompetence' in Blom-Cooper, L. (ed.), *After Beckford: Essays on Themes Connected with the Case of Jasmine Beckford.* London: Royal Holloway and Bedford New College.

Sheldon, B (2003) 'The risk of risks', *Evidence-based Social Care,* Autumn/Winter Issue, 15.

Sinclair, R (2001) referred to in Seden, J and others (2001) *Studies Informing the Framework for the Assessment of Children in Need and their Families.* The Stationery Office.

Stein, M and Hicks, L (2010) *Neglect Matters. A multiagency guide for professionals working together on behalf of teenagers.* Nottingham. DCSF.

Tompsett, H, Ashworth, M, Atkins, C, Bell, L, Gallagher, A, Morgan, M and Wainwright, P (2009) *The child and the family and the GP: Tensions and conflicts of interests in safeguarding children.* London: DCSF.

Treasure, J (2004) 'Motivational Interviewing', *Advances in Psychiatric Treatment,* 10, 331-337.

Tunnard, J (2002a) 'Parental drug misuse: A review of impact and intervention studies', *Research in Practice,* 2002.

Tunnard, J (2002b) 'Parental problem drinking and its impact on children', *Research in Practice,* 2002.

Tunnard, J (2004) 'Parental mental health problems messages from research policy and practice', *Research in Practice,* 2004.

Turnell, A and Edwards, S (1999) *Signs of Safety: A solution and safety orientated approach to child protection.* Norton and Co.

Turney, D, Platt, D, Selwyn, J and Farmer, E (2008) *Improving Child and Family Assessments: Turning research into practice.* London: Jessica Kingsley Publishers.

Turney, D, Platt, D, Selwyn, J and Farmer, E (2011) *Social Work Assessment of Children in Need: What do we know – Messages from research.* London: HMSO.

Velleman, R (2004) 'Alcohol and drug problems in parents: An overview of the impact on children and implications for practice' in Gopfert, M, Webster, J and Seeman, M, (2004) (eds) *Parental Psychiatric Disorder Distressed parents and their families.* Cambridge: Cambridge University Press.

Wald, MS and Woolverton, M (1990) 'Risk Assessment: The emperor's new clothes', *Child Welfare,* 69, 483-551.

Walker, S, Shemmings, D and Cleaver, H (2003) *Write Enough: Effective Recording in Children's Services* www.writeenough.org.uk

Ward, H, Brown, R, Westlake, D and Munro, E. (2010) *Infants suffering, or likely to suffer, significant harm: A Prospective Longitudinal Study.* Research Brief DFE-RB053. London: DFE.

Werner, EE (1971) *The Children of Kauai: A longitudinal study from the prenatal period to age ten.* Honolulu: University of Hawaii Press.

Werner, EE (1977) *Kaui's Children Come of Age.* Honolulu: Univesity of Hawaii Press.

Werner, EE (1982) *Vulnerable but invincible: a longitudinal study of resilient children and youth.* New York: McGraw-Hill.

Wiffin, J (2010) *The Children's Commisioner for England's report on Family Perspectives on Safeguarding and on relationships with Children's Services.* In-Trac Training and Consultancy.

Williams, A and McCann, J (2006) *Care Planning for Looked After Children: Guidance and training materials for multi-agency working* [CD-Rom]. London: National Children's Bureau.

Winnicott, C (1977) 'Communicating with children', *Social Work Today,* 8, 26.

Wolverhampton Safeguarding Children Board (2011) Executive Summary – Serious case review 2011: Child J (Ryan Lovell Hancox). Wolverhampton: Safeguarding Children Service.

Resources and useful information

This section includes ideas and suggestions of where to access reliable up-to-date information, including research findings, theory, literature reviews, overviews and training materials.

Many organisations have undertaken reviews of what is known about subjects pertinent to social work, such as the impact of domestic violence, the needs of learning disabled parents, or the outcomes for looked after children in a range of areas. They distil the huge amount of information already available into manageable reviews, which they often evaluate and update over time. These provide invaluable resources to agencies and practitioners who need to draw on such information but do not have time to trawl through it all themselves.

Useful contacts

Research in Practice (RiP)

The RiP website (www.rip.org.uk) provides many resources to assist people in accessing research reviews, and evaluations of them, on a broad range of relevant subjects. It also has, along with many other useful functions, the EvidenceBank.

RiP has also developed, from their Change projects, the following tools for agencies and teams to draw on when working towards reviewing and improving their ability to support evidence-based practice.

- *REAL* Organisational Support for Evidence-based Practice development project.

- TEAMWISE: Using research and evidence. The handbook produced from this project can be ordered from the website and has 21 tools in it to assist teams in developing practice.

RiP commenced a Change project on critical thinking and analysis in assessment in 2009 and published a literature review with the same title that year.

Further information on these can be accessed from the RiP website (above).

Making Research Count

This is a national collaborative research dissemination initiative, currently run by ten regional centres based in the Universities of East Anglia; Brighton; Keele; Luton; King's College, London; Nottingham; Salford; The Open University; Warwick; and York. This consortium of universities has a proven track record in social work and social care research, as well as providing social work education at qualifying and post-qualifying levels. These ten universities work in partnership with over sixty local authorities, NHS Trusts and other agencies, with a view to:

- promoting knowledge-based, research-informed practice

- improving the dissemination of research

- strengthening the research-mindedness and critical appraisal skills of social work and social care practitioners.

The Making Research Count website can be accessed at: http://www.uea.ac.uk/swk/ MRC_web/ public_html/

The Oxford Centre for Research into Parenting and Children

This multi-disciplinary centre brings together researchers in the University of Oxford, as well as researchers nationally and internationally with whom they have worked, who are researching into issues relating to parenting and children.

The aims of the centre are:

- to develop a better understanding of the well-being of parents and children; what causes problems (health, educational and social); and how they may be ameliorated

- to build multi-disciplinary, national and international research links

- to act as a discussion forum for researchers from different disciplines and for practitioners (health, education and social) who work with children and families

- to disseminate research findings.

The centre website contains links to the work of a number of researchers, including Dr Ann Buchanan who is the centre director, Dr David Jones and Kathy Sylva. www.apsoc.ox.ac.uk/ parenting

Social Care Institute of Excellence

The is another useful source of information, running specific networks such as the Parental Mental Health and Child Welfare Network, conducting knowledge reviews (so called because they often include not only literature overviews, but views and input from practitioners and users as well) and a website with a number of useful links and functions. www.scie.org.uk

Children's Commissioner

The office of the Children's Commissioner for England frequently produces reports, often in consultation with children and young people. For example: *Don't make assumptions: Children and young people's views of child protection* (March 2011) and *Trying to get by: Consulting with children and young people on poverty* (March 2011). More information can be found at www.childrenscommissioner.gov.uk

C4EO

The centre for excellence and outcomes in children and young people's services, C4EO, provides a range of products and support services to improve outcomes. For the first time, excellence in local practice, combined with national research and data about 'what works' is being gathered in one place. C4EO shares this evidence and the best of local practice with all those who work with and for children and young people and provides practical 'hands-on support' to help local areas make full use of this evidence. C4EO focuses on several themes including safeguarding and vulnerable children. Recent publications include:

- *Effective practice to protect children living in 'highly resistant' families knowledge review (March 2010)*

- *Effective interventions where there are concerns about, or evidence of, a child suffering significant harm. Briefing 1 (November 2009)*

- *What are the key questions for audit of child protection systems and decision-making. Briefing 2 (November 2009)*

CWDC

The Childrens Workforce Development Council, CWDC, was set up and funded by government to drive the development of the children and young people's workforce. They are responsible for developing the qualifications framework, quality standards, recruitment processes. One of CWDC's initiatives, The Newly Qualified Social Worker programme, contains useful handbooks for practitioners, including a supervisors' handbook that includes an examination of issues relating to supervision of child protection practice.

These can be downloaded from their website. www.cwdcouncil.org.uk

Membership organisations

Membership organisations, such as the following, also provide information and summaries of topics in various forms.

National Children's Bureau (NCB), at www.ncb.org.uk publish a series of research summaries in *Highlights*, available from NCB Online Bookshop, www.ncb.org.uk/books

Parenting UK, at www.parentinguk.org has information aimed at professionals who work with parents, including publications and briefings.

Barnardo's, at www.barnardos.org.uk has research and publications available to purchase or download, including the *What Works* series.

National Society for the Prevention of Cruelty to Children (NSPCC), at www.nspcc.org. uk has publications, information, leaflets, links and research studies available, including the NSPCC Inform service.

Drugscope, at www.drugscope.org.uk provides a library and information service; and has journals, and directories of information about drugs and of services.

Office of the United Nation's High Commissioner for Human Rights, at www.ohchr.org provides information about human rights issues including children's rights under the UN Convention as well as access to relevant links and publications.

Contact a Family, at www.contactafamily.org.uk is a UK-wide charity providing support, advice and information for families with disabled children. They also operate a helpline on 0808 808 3555 on Mondays from 10-4 and 5-7 and from Tuesday–Fridays between 10am and 4pm.

National Association for the Care and Resettlement of Offenders at www.nacro.org.uk is a crime reduction charity. The website contains information about their services in addition to information leaflets, briefings and publications about aspects of working with offenders, for example Looked After young people who offend or people with mental health problems.

The National Institute of Mental Health in England (NIMHE), at www.nimhe.org.uk, lists publications and resources; provides links, for example, to the Mental Health Research Network; and provides articles on current plans and activities.

Joseph Rowntree Foundation, at www.jrf.org.uk, provides a bookshop and findings from research projects.

Library and Information services can be accessed including text access to journals at: www.swetswise.com/direct.do

and at the British Library Inside service at www.inside.bl/user/secure/logon/do

Government websites

These websites provide access to guidance, publications and policy documents.

Department of Health – www.dh.gov.uk

Department for Education – www.education.gov.uk

Social Exclusion Unit – www.socialexclusion.gov.uk

Home Office – www.homeoffice.gov.uk

Local Government Information Unit – www.lgiu.gov.uk

Office for National Statistics – www.statistics.gov.uk

Sure Start – www.surestart.gov.uk

Further reading

Burton, Sheryl (1997) *When There's A Will There's A Way: Refocusing child care practice – A guide for team managers.* NCB.

Chaffin, M, Wherry JN, Newlyn, C, Crutchfield, A and Dykman, R (1997) 'The abuse dimensions inventory: Initial data on a research measure of abuse severity', *Journal of Interpersonal Violence*, 12, 4, August, 569–89.

City of Salford Community and Social Services (2000) *Conducting Family Assessments: A practice guide.* Russell House Publishing.

Directors of Social Work in Scotland (1992) *Child Protection: Policy, practice and procedure.* Edinburgh: HMSO.

Dowie, J and Elstein, A (1998) *Professional Judgement: A reader in clinical decision-making.* Cambridge University Press.

Dufour, S and Chamberland, C (2004) 'The effectiveness of selected interventions for previous maltreatment: Enhancing the well-being of children who live at home', *Child & Family Social Work*, 9, 39–56.

Fenman Ltd (2003) 'The definitive guide to creating a great learning experience', *Train the Trainer*, 1–25, 2003–2005.

Flynn, R (2000) 'Kinship foster care', *Highlight*, 179.

Gigerenzer, G, Todd, PM and ABC Research Group (1999) *Simple Heuristics that Make us Smart.* Oxford University Press, 3–33.

Gopfert, Webster, J and Seeman, Mary V (eds) (2004) *Parental Psychiatric Disorder: Distressed parents and their families.* Cambridge University Press.

Gorin, S (2004) *Understanding What Children Say: Children's experiences of domestic violence, parental substance misuse and parental health problems.* NCB.

Henniker, J, Print, B and Morrison, T (2002) An inter-agency assessment framework for young people who sexually abuse: Principles, processes and practicalities. *Child Care in Practice*, 8, 2.

Holt, R, Grundon, J and Paxton, R (1998) 'Specialist assessment in child protection proceedings: Problems and possible solutions', *Child Abuse Review*, 7, 266–79.

Jack, G, and Gill, O (2003) *The Missing Side of the Triangle: Analysing the influence of wider family and environmental factors on parenting and child development.* Barkingside: Barnardo's.

Kearney, P, Levin, E, and Rosen, G (2003) *Alcohol, drug and mental health problems: Working with Families.* SCIE.

Madge, N (2001) *Understanding Difference: The meaning of ethnicity for young lives.* NCB.

Madge, N, Burton, S, Howell, S and Hearn, B (2000) *The Forgotten Years: 9–13.* NCB.

Newman, T and Blackburn, S (2002) *Interchange 78: Transitions in the Lives of Children and Young People – Resilience Factors.* Scottish Executive Education Dept.

Randall, J, Cowley, P and Tomlinson, P (2000) 'Overcoming barriers to effective practice in child care. *Child and Family Social Work*, 5, 343–52.

Reder, P and Lucey, R (eds) (1995) *Assessment of Parenting: Psychiatric and psychological contributions.* Routledge.

Reder, P, Duncan, S, and Lucey, C (eds) (2003) S*tudies in the Assessment of Parenting.* Brunner-Routledge.

van Nijnatten, C, van den Ackerveken, M and Ewals, T (2004) 'Managing assessment quality planning in assessment procedures of the Dutch Child Protection Board', *British Journal of Social Work*, 34, 531–40.

Ward, H and Rose, W (eds)(2002) *Approaches to Needs Assessment in Children's Services.* London: Jessica Kingsley.

Walker, S (2003) *Social Work and Child and Adolescent Mental Health.* Russell House Publishers.

Webb, S (2001) 'Some considerations on the validity of evidence-based practice in social work', *British Journal of Social Work*, 31, 57–79.

Resources to improve communication with disabled children

In My Shoes is a computer package that helps children and adults with learning disabilities communicate their views, wishes and feelings as well as potentially distressing experiences. Further information from http://www.inmyshoes.org.uk/index.html

My Life, My Decisions, My Choice is a set of resources to aid and facilitate decision-making including a poster, set of laminated ring bound cards and a guide for professionals. The resources, produced by The Children's Society were designed with disabled young people and are aimed at young people, and the professionals that work with them. Available in hard copy from The Disability Advocacy Project, Telephone 020 7613 2886, or free to download from: http://sites.childrenssociety.org.uk/disabilitytoolkit/about/resources.aspx

How it is consists of an image vocabulary for children about feelings, rights and safety, personal care and sexuality. The vocabulary comprises 380 images that are designed to be used as a flexible resource to support children to communicate about their feelings, bodies, rights and basic needs. The pack includes a booklet and CD ROM. More information is available from www.howitis.org.uk

Available to purchase from: NSPCC Publications and Information Unit, NSPCC, 42 Curtain Road, London EC2A 3NH. Tel: 020 7825 2775. Email infounit@nspcc.org.uk